Indigeneity in the
Mexican Cultural Imagination

Indigeneity in the Mexican Cultural Imagination

THRESHOLDS OF BELONGING

Analisa Taylor

the university of arizona press   tucson

The University of Arizona Press
© 2009 The Arizona Board of Regents
All rights reserved
First issued as a paperback edition 2013

www.uapress.arizona.edu

Library of Congress Cataloging-in-Publication Data
Taylor, Analisa, 1969–
  Indigeneity in the Mexican cultural imagination :
thresholds of belonging / Analisa Taylor. p.   cm.
   Includes bibliographical references and index.
   ISBN 978-0-8165-2718-2 (cloth : alk. paper)
   ISBN 978-0-8165-3066-3 (pbk : alk. paper)
      1. Indians of Mexico—Public opinion. 2. Public opinion—Mexico.
3. Indians of Mexico—Government relations. 4. Indigenous peoples—
Mexico—Ethnic identity. I. Title.
F1219.3.P87T395   2009
305.897′07209045—dc22   2008053318

Earlier versions of some segments of this work have appeared in *Latin
American Literary Review, Journal of Latin American Cultural Studies,* and
Signs: Journal of Women in Culture and Society.

Manufactured in the United States of America on acid-free, archival-quality
paper and processed chlorine free.

18   17   16   15   14   13   7   6   5   4   3   2

Love makes us take off masks we fear we cannot live without, yet
know we cannot live within.

—James Baldwin

Contents

List of Figures   ix

Acknowledgments   xi

Introduction   1

1   Applied Anthropology and Post-revolutionary State
Consolidation   12

2   Narrating the Indian as Other: Foundational Indigenista
Fictions   25

3   The Ethnographic Coming-of-age Story   39

4   Testimonio and Indigenous Struggles for Autonomy   67

5   From Malinche to Matriarchal Utopia: Gendered and Sexualized
Visions of Indigeneity   82

Conclusion   105

Notes   117

Bibliography   125

Index   139

Figures

Women bearing gifts at a *vela*   83

Mayordomos at a vela in San Blas Atempa   86

Manuel embroiders   91

Cortés and la Malinche   98

Franciscan Monk   99

Cultural Diversity in Mexico   106

Acknowledgments

I am grateful for the inspiration and insights from my students and mentors as well as the support of family and friends who have sustained me throughout the writing of this book. A Foreign Language Area Studies Academic Research Abroad Fellowship allowed me to conduct initial research. The Graduate School and the Department of Romance Studies at Duke University provided steady financial support and intellectual stimulation. Faculty Research Awards from the College of Arts and Sciences and the Center for the Study of Women in Society (CSWS) at the University of Oregon as well as a National Endowment for the Humanities Summer Institute dedicated to "Mesoamerica and the Southwest: New Histories for an Ancient Land" provided crucial writing support. The book's content draws upon relationships I have cultivated at Duke University, the Colegio de México, and the University of Oregon, as well as with researchers in Oaxaca and Chiapas. I thank John Lie, who introduced me to the concept of race as a discourse and demonstrated its historical genesis in undergraduate sociology courses. Professors Barbara May, Luis Verano, Kay Kruger-Hickman, Juan Epple, and Amanda Powell have been outstanding models of intellectual inquiry for many years and have helped me to find my way as a scholar. I thank Alberto Moreiras, my dissertation advisor, for his rigorous mentorship and for the care with which he read and commented on the earliest shards of this work. I thank Susan Willis, Stephanie Sieburth, Gabriela Nouzeilles, and Sibylle Fischer for sharing valuable critical insights and providing steady encouragement. Ana María Alonso lent key insights into indigenismo and cultural nationalism in Mexico. Special thanks go to Cynthia Steele and José Rabasa, who read and commented extensively on earlier drafts of this book. Their contributions helped me to complete it. Deep gratitude goes to my colleague Gabriela Martínez, who advised and encouraged me as I revised much of this book. Though I am responsible for the book's shortcomings,

Gabriela deserves a great deal of credit for its strengths. I am indebted to Rafael Olea Franco, Rodolfo Stavenhagen, Rosalba Aída Hernández Castillo, Carlos Montemayor, Natividad Gutiérrez, Claudio Lomnitz, Roger Bartra, Salomon Nahmad, Margarita Dalton, Carlos Lenkersdorf, and Jesús Morales Bermúdez for their invaluable insights and guidance as I conducted research in Mexico. I am especially grateful to Marina Meneses and Susana Sánchez Vázquez for treating me like family in Juchitán and sharing their knowledge of Isthmus culture with me. I thank Jonathan Warren for inviting me to present part of this work at the University of Washington. I thank Patti Hartmann at the University of Arizona Press for the care and attention she has given this book at every stage and Tanya Grove for her meticulous copyediting. Bouquets of gratitude go to Barbara Altmann, Karen McPherson, Gina Herrmann, Mary Fechner, Lise Nelson, Amalia Gladhart, Irmary Reyes-Santos, Tania Triana, Stephanie Wood, Lynn Stephen, Carlos Aguirre, Lamia Karim, David Vázquez, Lynn Fujiwara, Ernesto Martínez, Eugene Gogol, Kristin Pesola, Katie McLean, Tracy Devine Guzmán, Victor Vich, Fabiola Orquera, Melissa Simmermeyer, Ryan Long, Freya Schiwy, Trent Hill, Yolanda Chávez-Leyva, Barbara Sutton, Mary Long, Miguel López, Diane Lewis, Roberto Arroyo, Blanca Aranda, Ana Paulina Mross, and Magalí Rabasa for offering feedback, encouragement, and friendship. I am grateful to Mary Dodge Smith, Gisela Bergman, Carmelita Thompson, and Susan Levine-Friedman; to my book group sisters—Chava Benin, Sarah Petersen, BJ Hurwich, Jan Wagner, and Annie Greenberg; and to all the great folks in my neighborhood for bringing balance and community to my life. Finally, thanks go to my family: gracias a mis suegros Teodoro y Socorro, mi cuñado Juan y mis cuñadas María Esther, Rosa María y Josefina por todo el apoyo y el cariño. Deep thanks go to my mother, Renee Nelson, for smoothing the edges around my life, for creating beauty in this world, and for encouraging me to find my own path. Thanks to my aunt, Dena Taylor, for giving me a writing refuge when I most needed it and for celebrating my progress. Thanks to my cousins Becky Taylor and Anna Olausson for their love and support. My husband, Pedro Perez, has shared insights on Mexican culture and politics that have shaped this book in countless ways, and has listened, read, commented, formatted, and reformatted with the patience and optimism that I often lacked.

I dedicate this book to you, Pedro, for you make me whole, and to our son Xavier, who has blessed our life together with new joy and purpose. With the two of you I have learned to greet each night dancing and to greet each day singing. And this book is for you, Leilani, first mother of our son and true sister of my heart.

*Indigeneity in the
Mexican Cultural Imagination*

Introduction

When Comandante Esther of the Zapatista Army of National Liberation (EZLN) addressed the National Congress in Mexico City in 2001, after facing extreme hostility from the right–wing National Action Party (PAN), she sketched a painfully stark portrait of indigenous women's place in national society: "The *mestizos* [mixed-race] and the wealthy mock us indigenous women because of our way of dressing, of speaking our language, our way of praying and of curing, and for our color, which is the color of the earth we work. We, in addition to being women, are indigenous, and as such, we are not recognized."[1] Comandante Esther stated that she was not approaching the political process as a Zapatista, but as an indigenous woman, an identity that for her is synonymous with the poorest of the poor. This speech highlights a crucial moment at which the Zapatista leadership, formed by Mayan men and women, revealed itself as the testimonial voice behind the ubiquitous subcomandante Marcos, the urbane and charismatic mestizo intellectual turned EZLN spokesman and translator. Comandante Esther's speech marks the first time an indigenous woman stood in the Palacio Legislativo to speak about the confluence of institutionalized racism, sexism, and poverty in Mexico. Today, along with Comandante Esther, a growing number of indigenous leaders and their non-indigenous collaborators are questioning racial and gender ideologies that have kept the indigenous—and particularly indigenous women—objectified as cultural icons of national identity yet marginalized from political processes directly affecting their well-being.

This moment is emblematic of how indigenismo has ceased to hold a monopoly in the marketplace of ideas about what it means to be indigenous in Mexico. I use the term *indigenismo* to refer to a social scientific paradigm wedded to a set of government institutions and policies as well as an aesthetic sensibility that has shaped a great deal of twentieth century Mexican art and literature. This book is about how the concept of "Indian" has been constructed as both a national ideal and a national problem in post-revolutionary Mexican indigenismo, as well as how that concept has been transformed in the neoliberal aftermath of national popular state formation. I examine how indigeneity has been defined, by whom, and to what ends in order to show not only how indigenous peoples have resisted marginalization, but also how that marginalization has often been perpetuated by the very individuals and institutions that have claimed an interest in indigenous peoples' welfare.

I aim to show not only how indigenismo constructs ethnicity and national identity from outside indigenous peoples' experiences, but also how these constructions are continually subverted by those cast as objects rather than protagonists of national renewal. Beneath the surface of much writing, both in the social sciences and literature, we find instances in which indigenous and non-indigenous interlocutors form subversive alliances to challenge indigenismo's central tenet that indigenous people must be assimilated to national culture in order to belong to the nation as full citizens. As early as the 1950s, *indigenista* literary and ethnographic works feature first-person oral accounts by indigenous speakers. As these indigenous narrator-informants talk back to their non-indigenous interlocutors, they introduce two crucial elements left out of official indigenista discourse and policy: indigenous subjectivity and indigenous resistance. The indigenous protagonists and shapers of these proto-testimonial narratives decry the chronic landlessness, hunger, and migration among indigenous communities that result from systematic discrimination by rural oligarchies acting in concert with the post-revolutionary state.

As Claudio Lomnitz observes, from roughly 1940 to 1982, the Institutional Revolutionary Party (PRI) cultivated spaces where intellectuals would "interpret 'national sentiment' on the basis of highly ritualized political manifestations by social groups that had little direct access to the media of national representation and debate" (2001, 114). Within this context of state-controlled intellectual life, indigenismo emerged as the dominant paradigm through which indigenous people were dealt with by the state. Indigenista theorists, practitioners, artists, and fiction writers often cast indigenous peasants as wards of the state in need of rescue from debt, peonage, and ignorance. In turn, they cast the post-revolutionary state as the Indians' defender against a retrograde and parasitic rural oligarchy out of touch with modern Mexican society.

In contemporary Latin America, indigenismo is generally understood in two related ways: first, it connotes the idea that indigenous people should be included in the mainstream of modern national life; second, it refers to a literary and visual mode that projects a romantic, folkloric image of the Indian as stoic, abject, and mysterious. In indigenista art and literature, indigenous people are depicted as if stuck at the threshold between a timeless, remote world and the everyday world of unfolding history. Thus, indigenismo racializes the dichotomy between traditional and modern life and frames the conditions under which people are included in or excluded from the nation. As a way of seeing Latin American society, indigenismo grafts this binary opposition between past and present onto ethnic differences, casting the Indian as a residual figure—an anomaly—and the mestizo as a modern citizen. The dichotomy effaces the existence of ethnic differences among indigenous groups and among other groups whose identities fall outside the Indian past/mestizo present binary. This leaves the many Latin Americans of African, Asian, Jewish, and Middle Eastern descent, as well as other groups, entirely out of the equation of Latin American culture.

Through homogenization, both ethnic and cultural, and indigeneity, which has been fictionalized and flattened, the ruling party in Mexico uses indigenismo to further national integration, while giving itself the role of revolutionary benefactor. As a social institution, a discourse of knowledge, and an aesthetic sensibility, indigenismo equates *mestizaje* with modernization and social equality. It equates indigeneity with remoteness and social stagnation, casting the Indian as *other*, within, yet always external to, the nation. While the mestizo is constructed as male and as the symbol of national unity, modernization, and progress, the Indian is depicted as feminine, fertile, and inert, likened to the productive agricultural landscape. The Indian symbolizes a work-in-progress, an object of the ever-unfolding post-revolutionary task of cultural and economic modernization.

State-sponsored Indigenismo: From Revolution to Rehabilitation

The National Indigenist Institute (Instituto Nacional Indigenista or INI) was conceived under President Lázaro Cárdenas in 1940 and formally inaugurated as a government agency by President Miguel Alemán in 1948. As the doors opened to its first Regional Coordinating Center in San Cristóbal de las Casas, Chiapas in 1950, indigenismo's revolutionary founding principles—bilingual education, ambitious land redistribution, and cooperative land ownership according to traditional indigenous laws and norms (*usos y costumbres*)—were replaced by a singular focus on assimilating indigenous people to Spanish-speaking, commercially oriented national society. Post-1930s indigenista action was predicated on the notion that indigenous peoples needed to be acculturated as a precondition for full citizenship. Remade as modern, individualistic mestizos, Indians would finally be entitled to the revolutionary fruits of social justice and modernization.

INI architect Alfonso Caso defined Indians not as a class, but as a mass, not yet ready to join the national political arena as either peasants or as workers.[2] Within the Mexican School of Anthropology that Caso helped found, indigeneity was defined in the narrowest of terms; only monolingual speakers of indigenous languages were considered indigenous. As director of the INI from 1948 until his death in 1970, Caso designed the INI as an agency from which to gather knowledge about different indigenous communities; this knowledge would then be used to assimilate these groups to national culture. As many critics of state-sponsored indigenismo in Mexico have noted, the policies designed by Caso and later refined by Gonzalo Aguirre Beltrán have had other implicit functions, namely that of creating mechanisms through which the single-party state could control indigenous peoples' land, labor, and civic relations, making them increasingly dependent on and beholden to the state and commercial interests outside their regions (Warman, 1970; Medina and García Mora, 1983; Díaz Polanco, 1996; Sánchez, 1999).

In ethnographic and fictional texts as well as visual arts and film, sexualized and infantilized stereotypes of "the Indian" have fed upon and fed into the government's indigenista practices. At the same time, theories and policies of induced cultural change elaborated within the INI have fostered a dualistic idea of the Indian as at once an ideal symbol of national identity (the virile pre-Conquest Aztec warrior) and a being whose inclusion in national society must be deferred (a female victim of Spanish colonization, la Malinche). As Héctor Díaz Polanco has noted, this ambivalent status, symbolically exalted yet socially marginalized, points to the racist conflation of an unsavory colonial past with indigenous identity itself. Hence, for indigenistas, it became the survival of indigenous peoples *as such*, rather than the survival of social structures inherited from colonial times that were considered to inhibit Mexico's development (1987, 42).

From Indigenismo to Indigenous Testimonio

In May 2003, President Vicente Fox closed the doors of the INI and inaugurated a new, smaller agency, the National Council for the Development of Indigenous Communities (Consejo Nacional para el Desarollo de los

Pueblos Indígenas or CONADEPI). With this change, the National Action Party (Partido Acción Nacional or PAN) buried the post-revolutionary state's traditional role as paternal figure delivering modernization and social justice to marginalized indigenous communities. The INI was shut down under the PAN because governing elites favored global market integration and hence, had no interest in social programs aimed to bring indigenous communities into the national economy and political system. Under current President Felipe Calderón, what we have is a relatively inconsequential bureau whose primary function is cosmetic, demonstrating that the Mexican government is honoring the multicultural foundations of Mexican society and simultaneously acting to contain rather than address social unrest.

Yet despite the waning of indigenista discourse and policy in recent years, mainstream political culture continues to be characterized by racism and the rationalization of glaring social inequalities between indigenous and non-indigenous society. Fossilized ideas about indigenous cultural backwardness continue to mask entrenched structures of socioeconomic, cultural, and political disenfranchisement. As a top-down prescription for incorporation of indigenous people into national society, indigenismo has become obsolete within the current neoliberal political order. Nevertheless, its narrow yet shifting definitions of what it means to be indigenous and what it means to be modern continue to determine the grounds on which indigenous and popular demands are managed in formal political processes. We can see this problem most acutely when we consider federal and state governments' responses to movements such as the Zapatista Army of National Liberation (EZLN) in Chiapas since 1994 and the Popular Assembly of the People of Oaxaca (APPO) since 2006. The government has refused to recognize any indigenous leadership within these movements, yet has targeted indigenous communities with military and paramilitary repression and silence.

Globalization and the Rearticulation of Indigeneity in Mexico

In 1992, in order to prepare Mexico for compliance with the North American Free Trade Agreement (NAFTA) set to take effect in 1994, President Carlos Salinas de Gortari stood under a larger-than-life-size painting of Emiliano Zapata and formally declared his modifications to Constitutional Article 27. This article or amendment had established the state as the owner of land, water, forests, and mineral resources and gave it the power to limit private ownership and break up existing large estates in order to grant land to collective, non-transferrable owners or *ejidatarios* (Bardacke, 1995, 267).

With Salinas's doctoring of the Constitution and signing of NAFTA, the PRI abandoned its carefully crafted image of itself as deliverer of revolutionary justice to the country's land-poor indigenous and mestizo peasants. As the self-named Party of the Revolution reversed property ownership laws and dismantled price controls on basic agricultural products, small-scale farmers became economic refugees within their own country and increasingly risked life and limb to seek work as undocumented migrants in *el norte*. As a result, toward the end of the twentieth century, the Mexican government forfeited the country's food sovereignty. Cheap corn and other basic foodstuffs from the U.S. heartland flooded the Mexican market (Barry, 1995). Land foreclosures, outmigration, military repression, and drug trafficking became the hungry new face of rural Mexico, particularly in the mountainous South and Southeast. Already suffering from the chronic effects of decades of failed agrarian reform policies, indigenous peasants in these regions felt the sting of neoliberalism most acutely. Yet this dramatic departure from the project of revolutionary nationalism was not as sudden as it may have appeared, but was preceded by a decade of dismantling of the cultural, educational, and social welfare programs that had lent a veneer of domestic stability and international credibility to the PRI throughout its nearly seventy-year rule.

Not coincidentally, 1992 is also remembered as a watershed year for the mobilization of indigenous peoples in Mexico and throughout the Americas. While many Europeans and their descendants celebrated the five hundred year anniversary of the "encounter" between Spaniards and Indians, grassroots organizations inaugurated a new cycle of indigenous and popular resistance to colonial narratives and designs. Mexican indigenous leaders challenged textbook notions about what it meant to be indigenous, about who could speak for and about the indigenous, and ultimately, about what indigenous peoples were supposed to become in order to belong in Mexican society. In the wake of the dismantling of the Mexican single party state, indigenous leaders have led the way in critiquing neoliberalism and its economic and cultural consequences, taking up the vanguard of a new type of global social movement organized against transnational corporations and the interest groups such as the World Trade Organization that represent them in formal international relations.

While 1992 marks an important year in which the idea of indigenous sovereignty in the Americas gained newfound international consideration, indigenous leaders and their non-indigenous allies have a much deeper history of critiquing and subverting state policies and organizations. Since the 1970s in particular, Mexican indigenous organizers have forged important links with other social movements throughout the Americas. The 1974 International Indigenous Congress held in San Cristóbal de las Casas in Chiapas stands out as a key moment in which these groups began to create national and international alliances, connecting their local struggles for land and self-determination with emerging international indigenous and popular movements.

At this point, indigenismo—as a discourse of cultural knowledge, as a government institution, and as an aesthetic sensibility—has been eclipsed by new modes of representation and social formations created by and for indigenous people. The uniquely Latin American literary genre of testimonio has played a crucial role in bringing indigenous perspectives to the attention of non-indigenous audiences in Mexico and around the world. Indigenous *testimonios* have grown out of these popular movements that resist the government's coercive acculturation efforts as well as recent neoliberal policies that threaten the cultural and economic vitality of indigenous communities.

As the indigenous testimonios discussed in this book show, representations of indigeneity have changed most dramatically since the 1980s and 1990s. At this time, the ruling party state began to dismantle or neglect its costly web of institutions dedicated to understanding and controlling indigenous affairs. In the wake of state-sponsored indigenista cultural and social welfare projects, new types of cultural production and social organization created by indigenous and non-indigenous collaborators have emerged. Today, indigenous activists and their non-indigenous allies critique the ways in which indigenous cultural difference has been constructed to fit the exigencies of the state's development prerrogatives. As indigenous people seek out new avenues toward self-determination and empower themselves through activism, education, and collaborative forms of cultural production, they subvert dominant perceptions of race and culture and redefine what it means to be indigenous on radically new terms.

Chapter one "Applied Anthropology and Post-revolutionary State Consolidation" shows how indigenous identities are defined within government-sponsored social institutions from the 1940s to the 1980s. I examine indigenismo as an anthropological paradigm wedded to a government policy of ethnic assimilation carried out in the INI's regional coordinating centers. INI theorists and policy makers championed national cohesion and modernization through mestizaje, understood not as a mixture of two parts in equal measure, but as a genetic and cultural absorption and attenuation of indigenous into Hispanic traits. Throughout the period of post-revolutionary state consolidation, cultural and intellectual projects relating to the place of indigenous peoples within the nation have been restricted to a tightly knit constellation of non-indigenous intellectuals. Within a PRI-controlled framework, the "Indian problem" had been defined not as one of unfulfilled land, labor, and educational reforms, but of indigenous cultural backwardness. By considering indigenous culture to be the culprit for indigenous poverty and illiteracy, indigenismo turned a revolutionary project into a charitable one. It turned a problem of enduring structural inequalities into a problem of cultural maladjustment to the modern capitalist world.

Chapter two, "Narrating the Indian as Other: Foundational Indigenista Fictions," looks at indigenismo as a literary genre in vogue from the 1930s to the 1950s. Indigenista novels show how indigenous identity becomes a site of contradictory social prerogatives within the Mexican cultural imagination. Here, I focus on indigenismo as the fictionalization of indigenous life and consciousness by non-indigenous novelists. These writers adopt the role of amateur ethnographers, portraying the unique political, religious, and psychosocial dynamics of present-day indigenous communities. In other words, they create an exaggerated portrait of those aspects that make the indigenous characters seem authentic. The reader, in the act of consuming indigenista fiction, virtually accompanies the pseudo-ethnographer or narrator "across the threshold" on a fictional fieldwork expedition, swept up in a process of vicarious participant observation.

Three of these "foundational" indigenista novels fictionalize the relationship between the post-revolutionary state, indigenous peasants, and remnants of the pre-revolutionary Porfirian rural oligarchy. My analysis of character and plot development, as well as eroticized telluric imagery, in *El indio* (1935), by Gregorio López y Fuentes, *El resplandor* (1937), by Mauricio Magdaleno, and *Lola Casanova* (1943), by Francisco Rojas González, shows what official indigenista discourse seeks to conceal: the ambivalent consciousness of post-revolutionary national elites pursuing rural capitalist development under the benevolent guise of revolutionary social justice for indigenous peasants.

Chapter three, "The Ethnographic Coming-of-age Story" shows that in the 1950s and 1960s, ethnography and literature begin to mirror one another as each seeks to adopt a more "authentic" indigenous point of view. Fiction writers appropriate images from ethnographies and oral popular narrative forms. In turn, ethnographers influenced by structuralism and cultural relativism bring metaphor, plot development and narrative voice into their monographs as they attempt to reconstruct a community's sense of the world from the tape-recorded life stories of their indigenous informants.

While the overt purpose of indigenismo was to facilitate indigenous assimilation to Spanish-speaking mestizo society, that goal as prescribed by the INI necessarily began with listening to and gaining the cooperation of indigenous leaders (Aguirre Beltrán, 1990). The functionalist view of indigenous culture as static and hermetic that had predominated in the literary and ethnographic works of the 1920s to the 1940s did not serve the ends of indigenistas in the 1950s and beyond. These mid-century ethnographers saw indigenous assimilation to national culture as necessary and inevitable for modernization and social cohesion. They redefined Robert Redfield's folk or indigenous peasant community (Redfield, 1948) as mutable, and cast themselves as agents of indigenous assimilation.

In *Juan Pérez Jolote* (1952), by Ricardo Pozas, and *Los hombres verdaderos* (1959), by Carlo Antonio Castro, both authors cede partial authorial voice to the indigenous informants that animate their texts. Their ethnographic work takes a decidedly literary turn that anticipates later developments in post-modern ethnography and testimonio. These authors worked within the regional coordinating centers of the INI, living for extended periods among the indigenous groups they depicted in their narratives. Reading their fictionalized accounts of highland Maya life, we can see that their cultural fantasies were not so much of possession of indigenous land and labor, as had been the case in the earlier indigenista novels examined in chapter two, but of adoption of mestizo cultural norms and values. *Juan Pérez Jolote* and *Los hombres verdaderos* change the parameters of ethnographic discourse by placing the tape-recorded life stories of indigenous informants at the center of their narratives, blurring what had been a rigid boundary between subject and object, as well as between empirical evidence and literary conceit.

Another type of indigenista writing to emerge at this time, the ethno-historical novel, allowed fiction writers to borrow from what they had learned of indigenous storytelling traditions as well as retrace the conflicting historical memories of conquest and colonization from both indigenous and Spanish or *Criollo* perspectives. *Oficio de tinieblas* (1962), by Rosario Castellanos, fictionalizes the Highland Maya revolt of 1867. By situating this narrative in a fictional time that blends the colonial past with the 1930s, Castellanos subverts the claim made by Eurocentric historiography by creating temporal palimpsests and punctuating them with references to ancient books of Mayan prophesy such as the *Popol Vuh* and the *Libro de Chilam Balam de Chumayel*. By projecting her characters into intercultural spaces of conflict and solidarity between *ladino* (non-indigenous) and Indian society, she creates a psychological identification between the reader and the legendary indigenous rebel-heroes of this revolt. As Pozas and Castro do in their proto-testimonios, Castellanos explores the melding perspectives of indigenous and ladino characters gesturing toward the more overtly political writing of testimonio explored in the following chapter. Unlike Pozas and Castro, however, Castellanos focuses on relationships between women, exploring the complex intersections of racial and gender oppression.

Beginning with the First Inter-American Indigenous Congress in San Cristóbal de las Casas, Chiapas in 1974, grassroots indigenous-led organizations began to create a space of social critique and action outside the purview of the ruling party state. As chapter four, "Testimonio and Indigenous Struggles for Autonomy" discusses, indigenous leaders effectively recast the terms of debate regarding indigenous inclusion in national affairs. Emerging in the 1970s and 1980s and subject to continual transformations in the following decades, Mexican indigenous testimonios represent both a continuation and a subversion of previous indigenista literary and ethnographic forms. Indigenous and non-indigenous interlocutors began to share the authority from which to convey indigenous perspectives. I draw upon current theories of Latin American testimonio to demonstrate how testimonial writing has catalyzed indigenous struggles for self-determination in Mexico. The EZLN letters and communiqués penned by subcomandante Marcos are exemplary in their capacity to drum up national and international solidarity for groups vulnerable to military and paramilitary repression. However, there are important antecedents such as *Memorial del tiempo o vía de las conversaciones* (1987), by Jesús Morales Bermúdez, and *Entre anhelos y recuerdos* (1997), by Marie-Odile Marion, that help us to see these writings within a wider context of pluricultural literary production. Like the EZLN writings, these testimonios address relationships between patriarchal oppression and racism as well as the imbalance of power between themselves and their indigenous interlocutors. In Mexico, testimonios have been crucial in the construction of a shared, though problematic, space from which to speak about indigenous cultural survival in the context of global capitalist expansion.

Chapter five, "From Malinche to Matriarchal Utopia: Gendered and Sexualized Visions of Indigeneity" contrasts the indigenista vision of an abject indigenous femininity embodied in the historical figure of Malinche with representations of Zapotec women and muxes (gay or womanly men in Zapotec) in the Isthmus of Tehuantepec, Oaxaca. Within mestizo nationalist treatments, Malinche—Cortés's interpreter and consort in the sixteenth century conquest of Mexico—has been fashioned as the archetypal raped and scorned Indian mother of the modern mestizo nation.

Together, these alter-ego myths, of an abject indigenous femininity on one hand and an exalted indigenous femininity on the other, have fed into the negation of indigenous women's agency within mainstream discussions of national identity and political imperatives in Mexico. Although much of what we point to as evidence of matriarchy among Isthmus Zapotecs can be found in other parts of Mexico, we have been conditioned to see empowered Mexican women as the exception, to notice only the machismo that Octavio Paz and other intellectuals have considered synonymous with Mexican identity.

The conclusion considers whether the phenomena examined in the preceding chapters hold in a Mexico characterized by severe political and economic crises, such as those generated by allegations of electoral fraud in the 2006 presidential elections and repression of the popular movement to oust governor Ulises Ruíz in Oaxaca in the same year. The key question is whether indigenous reformulations of national belonging as a pluralistic, even dialogic endeavor will find effective avenues of expression within the neoliberal model of market-driven governance and cultural production. Has neoliberalism abolished the twentieth century's central narrative of a unified, ethnically homogeneous *pueblo*, or have its gravest contradictions brought that pueblo to perceive itself as multiethnic yet politically unified on radically new terms?

1

Applied Anthropology
and Post-revolutionary
State Consolidation

> The Indian blends into the landscape until he is an indistinguishable part
> of the white wall against which he leans at twilight, of the dark earth on
> which he stretches out to rest at midday, of the silence that surrounds
> him. He disguises his human singularity to such an extent that he finally
> annihilates it and turns into a stone, a tree, a wall, silence, and space.

This painterly image of "the Indian" as a stoic, indeed stone-like figure
in Octavio Paz's well-known portrait of modern Mexico, *The Labyrinth of
Solitude* (1950), exemplifies an indigenista literary sensibility. Because indigenous peoples speak languages that are incomprehensible to the author,
they are bestowed with an eloquent silence; because their being is unfath-
omable to him, they are depicted as hermetic and motionless, conspicuous
by virtue of their apparent invisibility. The somber elegance of this image
naturalizes a way of perceiving in which one does not have to know any
Indians to know exactly what "Indianness" is all about.

Paz's sketch is not an isolated instance of essentialism, nor is it without
political consequences. Indigenismo is not simply a set of aesthetic or literary conventions; nor is it exclusively a social scientific paradigm wedded
to official government institutions and policies. It is a discourse of cultural
knowledge that fashions the Mexican "Indian" as the post-revolutionary
state's moral obligation: a backward, infantile, and passive entity standing
in the way of modernization and progress. As a way of imagining Indians

as victims of history and objects of the non-Indian gaze, indigenismo has served to mystify popular revolutionary demands for land and liberty, and at the same time, to assuage persistent anxieties among ruling elites about peasant revolt.

The INI and National Popular State Consolidation

From its formal inauguration as a government bureau by President Miguel Alemán in 1948 until its official closing by President Vicente Fox in 2003, The National Indigenist Institute (Instituto Nacional Indigenista, INI) had functioned as the primary broker of the state's interests in indigenous communities.[1] The INI's explicit mission had been to alleviate inequality between white and mestizo society on one hand and indigenous society on the other, facilitating the emergence of a culturally and politically unified nation. By casting the problem of indigenous marginalization in these terms, however, indigenismo has set up a dichotomy between Indian and non-Indian society that whitewashes the ethnic complexity of Mexican society.

Other state institutions such as the National Institute of Anthropology and History (Instituto Nacional de Antropología e Historia, INAH) and the National School of Anthropology and History (Escuela Nacional de Antropología e Historia, ENAH) were enlisted to serve the aims of indigenista activities. The first specialized in recovering, archiving, and showcasing the relics of the pre-conquest past as the origins of the modern mestizo nation; the second focused on cultivating the expertise of future generations of indigenista theorists and practitioners.

Anthropologists, linguists, agronomists, and other specialists worked in concert with the INI to accomplish the following: study regional cultural enclaves, especially those in remote areas whose lifeways were perceived as obstacles to national modernization; and to propose, carry out, and evaluate infrastructural, social welfare, and pedagogical projects designed to hasten assimilation of these groups into the nation. While this comprehensive project aimed to bring indigenous peoples into Spanish-speaking mestizo society, it also served to channel indigenous peoples' participation in the national sphere in ways advantageous to the ruling party state. Indigenismo has been an important mechanism for consolidating the power of the Institutional Revolutionary Party (PRI) and delineating the parameters of modern national subjectivity.

Indigenistas working within these institutions championed national cohesion and modernization through mestizaje, defined as a genetic and cultural absorption and attenuation of indigenous into Hispanic traits. Within this post-revolutionary refashioning of national identity, to be mestizo was to be the protagonist of the Revolution of 1910, the primary agent of a vibrant present and future Mexico. To be indigenous was to inhabit a threshold between a local, static reality and a national, modern one.

The concept of indigenismo originally sprang from the Mexican Revolution as an affirmation that indigenous culture was the wellspring of modern national identity. As in Andean indigenismo in the 1920s and 1930s, early Mexican indigenistas sought to bring indigenous peoples into the mainstream of national life through public education and to model land reform on traditional indigenous systems of communal land tenure. Yet as Alexander S. Dawson notes, while these revolutionary indigenistas promoted assimilation of indigenous peoples into the nation, their inherited ideas about Indian racial inferiority, which were "rooted in four centuries of colonial domination and built on a series of polarities—the Christian versus the heathen, the *gente de razón* versus the savage, the masculine versus the feminine, and culture versus nature," got in the way of their project to create "a single Mexican community, defined by the political rights and obligations that they associated with citizenship in a modern nation"(2004, 4).

Indigenismo lost its revolutionary edge as it was brought under the direction of the federal government through the INI in the 1940s. In its privileging of mestizaje—as assimilation was not only of the Indian to the Hispanic, but also of the feminine to the masculine, the rural to the urban, and the traditional to the modern—indigenismo created a prescription for full citizenship that categorically excluded indigenous peoples as such. Its representations of indigenous peoples as abject, inert, and incomplete beings at the threshold of citizenship have cohered with the state's drive for economic and political control of the countryside in the latter two-thirds of the twentieth century.[2]

The Foundations of Official Indigenismo

In 1940, as President Lázaro Cárdenas's six-year term came to an end and Manuel Ávila Camacho prepared to succeed him, Cárdenas inaugurated the First Inter-American Indigenist Conference in Pátzcuaro, Michoacán. Attending the conference were diplomats and scientists from nineteen countries as well as forty-seven Indians representing twenty different tribes—thirty-two from Mexico, one from Panama, and fourteen from the United States. Its purpose was to establish a permanent Inter-American

Indigenist Institute (Instituto Indigenista Interamericana, III) to "serve as a clearing house for data relating to the Indians of the American republics."[3]

Participants drafted a series of resolutions with which to pressure North American and Latin American governments to adopt a hemisphere-wide Indian policy. However, these resolutions did not challenge the structure of power in the different countries, since ultimately they stressed that individual governments should make their own assessments and policy decisions based on their own interests. These resolutions urged governments concerned with the welfare of indigenous peoples to employ anthropologists and other experts in the implementation of their programs of social action. At the insistence of the delegation from the United States, the final declaration in this document is a disclaimer: approval of these resolutions does not force state governments to commit to them.[4] Thus, individual governments are reassured that indigenista programs pose no threat to the prevailing social structure. On the contrary, they legitimize the notion that national sovereignty ultimately rests not in the hands of citizens but in those of the nation's policy makers. Furthermore, these resolutions address the problem of concentration of land in the hands of an oligarchic minority, yet stop short of addressing the root causes of this problem: the colonial legacy of indigenous labor exploitation as well as land ownership by those of predominantly European descent.

Article I, regarding land tenure, is particularly notable for its ambivalence regarding the role of individual states in dealing with the concentration of wealth:

> In those nations where land is concentrated in the hands of a few, their respective governments should adopt the means necessary, according to equality and justice, to correct any abuses engendered by this situation; it also recommends that measures be taken that will be necessary to help their indigenous populations to improve their economies, providing them with land, water, credit, and technical assistance.[5]

Here, governments of the Americas are advised to "correct any abuses" that occur as a result of the concentration of land. The concentration of land is not itself the problem to be addressed directly. The problem to be ameliorated is simply "any abuses engendered by this situation." Although this resolution is titled "Land Distribution for the Indigenous," it makes only a passing mention of land distribution. The underlying suggestion is that while steps should be taken to better the social position of indigenous peoples, no radical change in the larger economic structure would be necessary to that end.[6]

In addition to these resolutions, each participating country was encouraged to establish a national Indian affairs bureau "to serve as a liaison agency for the central body."[7] It was in this pan-American spirit that the INI, along with similar institutes throughout Latin America, was created as a state agency.

These conference proceedings reflect the ideological contradictions that have accompanied indigenismo throughout its existence as a government project. On one hand, indigenistas advocate for a radical transformation of ethnic and class relations that would ultimately change the situation of indigenous peoples in Latin America. On the other, they promote state paternalism by positing that indigenous peoples need to be protected as minors, thus negating any presupposition of social transformation.

Herein lies the hegemonic relation set up through indigenismo: as it substitutes the terms "peasant" and "agrarian community" associated with revolutionary struggle with those of "Indian" and "indigenous community," associated now with the emerging paradigm of development and later, the Green Revolution, class antagonisms are redefined as cultural antagonisms. Benjamín Maldonado Alvarado notes that the drive to take away indigenous peoples' culture implies thinking that

> since the European invasion Indians ceased to be the shapers of their own history and became only refugees of it. It would follow, then, that as Indians live according to fragmented and inefficient cultures, they need to adopt the only culture that is culture: Western culture. . . . It is assumed that Indians keep being Indians not because they want to continue to be Indians, but because they have not been given the means that would allow them to cease to be Indians or because they are afraid of ceasing to be Indians. (17)

This paternalistic approach noted by Maldonado appears early on in official indigenista discourse; at the Inter-American Indigenista Conference's opening ceremony, President Cárdenas addressed participants as follows: "The incorporation of the Indian to modern civilization should not be carried out as an act of charity, but of justice."[8] In this statement "the Indian" is defined as a collective singular entity; hence, the difference between any two Indians is rendered insignificant when compared with the difference between all Indians and all non-Indians. By stating that "the Indian should be incorporated as an act of justice and not of charity," Cárdenas implies that whatever the ideological motivation—be it charity or justice—the fundamental *task* of incorporation into "modern civiliza-tion," here equated with mestizo culture, remains inevitable. Cárdenas implies that those who already belong to modern civilization should be the ones to accomplish this task. What is to be discussed—the objective of the conference participants—is to determine the spirit with which the task of incorporation is to be undertaken.

Among post-revolutionary presidents, Cárdenas worked most earnestly to fulfill the land reform and educational platforms of the 1917 Constitu-tion. However, he also established the foundation for the centralized, cor-poratist model of political organization that later became the PRI's greatest tool for maintaining its long-standing rule. Cárdenas modeled a brand of charismatic populist statesmanship that was later emulated by his more conservative successors. His dual legacy was to nationalize key industries such as petroleum and electricity as well as enact the most far-reaching agrarian reform of any post-revolutionary president. The vehicle for this reform was the *ejido*, or communal land tenure system, institutionalized by the agrarian reform program since 1915.[9]

However, another die had already been cast: Cárdenas had followed Presidents Carranza, Obregón, and Calles. These post-revolutionary rul-ers laid claim to their protagonism in the revolutionary struggle. Once in office, however, they protected landowners' interests by undercutting land reform. These presidents ensured that powerful landowners could almost always find one loophole or another that would exempt them from ceding their vast holdings.[10] According to Consuelo Sánchez:

> Carranza, Obregón and Calles waved the flag of agrarian reform as a political tool to accomplish other ends. While Carranza was in office, more than 200 thousand hectares, or one percent were distributed to peasant communities. After 1920, Obregón and Calles focused their efforts on creating an agrarian economy based on small or medium plots and on the hacienda, which they had no intention of eliminating. Calles went so far as to propose the cancellation of agrarian reform.[11] (Sánchez, 1999, 26)

Following Cárdenas' six-year term, Presidents Manuel Ávila Camacho and later Miguel Alemán further muted the socialist tenor of Cárdenas' programs while keeping his corporatist structure and populist rhetoric of revolutionary justice in place. At this point, the notion that peasants constituted a social class was politically dangerous to the government and the emerging national bourgeoisie. In order for these elites to control peas-ants' political agency, they needed to create a new set of identifications, based not on class but on culture. By embracing indigenismo, the state appropriated the image of revolution as peasant revolt, yet emptied it of its threatening content by downplaying the peasant struggle for land. It defined problems of social inequality as stemming not from these historical conflicts but from disadvantageous cultural traits.

Critique of Indigenismo

Under the direction of renowned archaeologist Alfonso Caso, the INI exercised a virtual monopoly on the field of social scientific production and functioned as an extension of the state's interests in indigenous communities. Drawing upon José Vasconcelos's and Manuel Gamio's theories of national identity, Caso and other architects of official indigenismo created a complex mechanism through which political subjectivity was tied to ethnicity rather than class.

Gonzalo Aguirre Beltrán, one of the principle theorists and administrators of indigenista action, designated indigenous enclaves in need of development as hinterlands or "refuge regions." In these refuge regions, Aguirre Beltrán oversaw the creation of the INI's coordinating centers that served anthropologists, agronomists, engineers, and other professionals as bases from which to implement government-funded projects such as the construction of rural schools, roads and transportation networks, health clinics, and other programs. These programs were designed to foment indigenous integration into the national economy, language, and culture. Ethnographers and linguists used the regional coordinating centers as bases for researching the languages and cultural practices of the indigenous communities. In turn, the information gathered by specialists was used to fine-tune the theoretical apparatus and to expand the INI's development projects in various regions throughout Mexico (Aguirre Beltrán, 1993).

Ultimately, as Aguirre Beltrán pointed out, the INI and related institutions had to answer to the government. In his plans for indigenous acculturation, he indicated that the director of the INI "meets periodically with the president of the Republic in order to assure concordance with the national political agenda."[12] Thus, the theoretical and practical directions taken by the INI were ultimately determined by the objectives of the federal government.

Beginning in the 1960s and 1970s, social scientists (many of whom worked within the INI and other government agencies) and indigenous leaders charged that behind the moral veneer of enlightened acculturation touted by indigenista ideologues, the state was engaged in a project of dismantling indigenous peoples' traditional, self-sufficient peasant economies in order to secure political and economic control of the countryside. They argued that indigenismo had morally exhausted itself, torn as it was by the contradiction between its egalitarian promise and its homogenizing practice. When the state unleashed brutal repression against its citizens in the late 1960s and 1970s, indigenismo began to lose credibility among many of its theorists and practitioners. The 1968 massacre in the Plaza de Tlatelolco in Mexico City, in which over four hundred students and sympathizers were killed, is a moment when the rift between the state and its citizens becomes brutally clear. At the same time, intellectuals questioned how anthropology had constructed indigenous identity from a Eurocentric perspective. These critics claimed that indigenismo was not bettering the conditions of indigenous peoples but rather, had served to incorporate them into a situation of increased dependency. In *La imagen del indio en el discurso del Instituto Nacional Indigenista* (The Image of the Indian in the Discourse of the National Indigenist Institute, 1992) Consuelo Ros Romero elaborates on Carlos Medina's concern with the ethics of indigenismo:

> The most important year in the period of crisis in Mexican indigenismo was 1968. The student movement and concerns about American anthropology's relationship to colonialist expansion were echoed in Mexico. This critique, focused on the National School of Anthropology and History (ENAH), "denounced Mexican anthropology's colonialism, the absence of critical positions by the majority of its representatives, as well as the reactionary character of its many contributions" (Medina 1973:23–24). The values behind [Mexican] anthropology, which date back to Cárdenas' time, are severely questioned: [from that point on,] it will be necessary to "rethink indigenista politics."[13]

Critics argued that by placing the emphasis on indigenous culture as the culprit for indigenous poverty and illiteracy, indigenismo turned a revolutionary project into a charitable one. Ideals that had previously accompanied debates on the place of indigenous culture within national society, such as bilingual education and indigenous self-determination, were banished after 1940.

Such critiques of the official indigenista paradigm gained greater momentum in the 1970s. The death of Alfonso Caso in 1970, the murder of peasant leader Lucio Cabañas by state police in Guerrero in 1973, and the First Inter-American Indigenous Conference held in San Cristóbal de las Casas, Chiapas in 1974 (which brought together indigenous leaders from throughout the Americas) all served to create a ripe environment for debate and action. At this point, the contradiction between indigenismo's egalitarian aims and its exploitative results emerged in the light of feminist, civil rights, and third world decolonization movements.[14]

Rodolfo Stavenhagen was among the first to point out that owing to the social sciences' intimate relationship with the ruling party state, discussions of class inequalities and racial discrimination had been suppressed from the social scientific establishment, impeding any understanding of real obstacles to social justice.[15] Guillermo Bonfil Batalla argued that while the explicit goal of indigenismo was development, its implicit goal and results amounted to ethnocide. He claimed that indigenismo's aim was to make indigenous peoples disappear as differentiated ethnic groups "in order to expand the internal market, to increase the labor supply and keep wages low and to incorporate the indigenous inhabitants of 'refuge regions' into the process of rationalized production" (Medina and Mora, 1983, 145–46).

Repression of peasant movements in the countryside brought a growing number of anthropologists and rural sociologists to condemn the premises and results of applied anthropology. They argued that despite its rhetoric of modernization predicated on ethnic homogeneity, the state had reneged on its revolutionary plan to end class inequality. These intellectuals concluded that institutionalized indigenismo, far from ameliorating the condition of indigenous peasants, had contributed to social demobilization following the populist reform of the 1930s.

As a political ritual of manipulating indigenous cultural identity, indigenismo has clearly turned a problem of fundamental social inequalities into a problem of indigenous cultural backwardness. Yet even as indigenismo has been phased out of state policy and has perhaps become a relic of the national popular era, the tensions these critics observed between the government and indigenous communities remain highly significant to us today.

As these critiques began to circulate among social scientists, indigenous peasants were organizing themselves against land foreclosures and manipulation by mestizo merchants and politicians. A collaborative relationship was developing between indigenous leaders involved in these new social movements and leftist intellectuals such as Salomón Nahmad and Araceli Burguete working to wrest some autonomy from the state's academic, social, and cultural establishments. This new generation of intellectuals who critiqued the institutions that had trained and employed them had to choose between preserving the initial revolutionary impulse behind indigenismo and abandoning it altogether in search of new modes of representation and models of social action.

Post-Indigenismo to Pan-Indianismo in the Neoliberal Era

Ros Romero demonstrates that with its increasing bureaucratization in the 1960s and 1970s, the INI intensified its focus on co-opting indigenous leaders and controlling community affairs while at the same time "focusing its discursive efforts on reporting or recounting its activities." According to Ros Romero, this discourse constructed a stereotype of "the Indian" and glorified the INI's achievements (1992, 106). At the same time, she explains, as indigenismo became engulfed in the state bureaucracy, its representation of indigenous peoples became increasingly tautological and its projects focused on the manipulation of indigenous communities for short-term political gain (118–19).

In 1982, upon defaulting on its massive international debt, the Mexican state promised to comply with the payment schedule set by the International Monetary Fund and World Bank as well as to take on neoliberal policies such as deregulating corporations and privatizing state-run industries and institutions. It radically scaled back its sponsorship of cultural and social welfare programs and abandoned its long-standing tutelary relationship with the poorest and most disenfranchised of its citizens, leaving them to do battle with the global market on their own (Nash, 2001; Hernández Castillo, 2001).

Today in Mexico, as throughout much of Latin America, the state no longer funds or controls educational and cultural institutions to the degree it once did, leaving the market as the sole arbiter of cultural value (Moreiras, 2001; G. Williams, 2002; Yúdice, 2003). The result in Mexico is that, at the beginning of the twenty-first century, the state has withdrawn much of its support for the many cultural and social programs aimed at integrating indigenous peoples into the nation. In turn, it has abandoned its carefully crafted narratives of modernization, revolutionary justice, and national belonging.

Pushed to the limits of subsistence by the increased burdens of foreign debt and vulnerability to world market–price fluctuations, today indigenous peasants feel the sting of these neoliberal policies most acutely. In this context, indigenous activists are seeking new avenues through which to recast the terms of debate regarding indigenous inclusion in national and international affairs.

Particularly since the neoliberal paradigm was formalized with the North American Free Trade Agreement (NAFTA) in 1994, the old vocabularies and images signifying "Indian" and "nation" have become obsolete. National popular mythologies of the meek Indian and the fatherly state are equally incongruent with the new cultural strategies indigenous communities are developing to cope with these structural changes. Instead of acquiescing or disassociating themselves from their communities of origin, many indigenous people in Mexico and throughout the Americas are rejecting essentialist definitions of indigeneity and forging a new type of identity politics. The emergence of bilingual indigenous literature, radio, video, theater, dance, music, and art attests to this new type of indigenous cultural politics (Montemayor and Frischmann,2004; Steele,1993; Underiner, 2004).

These new perspectives on indigenous cultural identity—and the new political subjectivities they mirror—have emerged at a time when significant social reorientations are taking place. On one hand, the Mexican ruling elite has moved progressively toward a political and economic model based on the privatization of major industries, massive cuts to social services, and a disengagement from public culture; on the other, indigenous groups are finding ways to enter and transform those very spheres of national culture and civic life vacated by official government institutions. This dynamic is present in Mexico as well as in other regions of Latin America where indigenous people form a significant segment of the population, particularly Bolivia, Peru, Ecuador, and Guatemala. Throughout the Americas, we find similar forms of indigenous cultural and political realignments.

As indigenous leaders challenge state hegemony and neoliberal policies, non-indigenous intellectuals have begun to approach their interlocutors with less paternalism and more humility. Disillusioned with government repression of popular protest, disenfranchised from market-driven intellectual life, and sympathetic with the cause of impoverished peasants, these intellectuals have used the uniquely Latin American genre of testimonio to give indigenous speakers a share in the authorship of knowledge produced in their name. The indigenous narrator-protagonists of these collaborative texts are presented to the reader as cognizant, empowered subjects rather than passive objects of empirical reflection or literary fascination. In this context, we can finally see that Paz's image of the silent, stoic Indian reveals more to us about dominant society's view of indigenous peoples than it does about the Indians he purports to represent.

When these testimonio writers begin to *listen to*—rather than simply *speak for*—indigenous peoples, a notable ambivalence about indigenismo's homogenizing gaze emerges in their work. As indigenous and non-indigenous voices meld and enter into dialogue in these testimonial texts, we can glimpse the limits of indigenismo and the stirrings of an alternate cultural formation, one in which indigenous peoples have a hand in shaping what it means to be Indian in contemporary Mexico.

The following chapters will contribute to our understanding of the cultural implications of the 1994 uprising of the Zapatista Army of National Liberation (EZLN) in Chiapas as well as other grassroots movements around the country. The Mayan EZLN comandantes affirm that to be indigenous is not to be a relic of a buried past, as so many twentieth-century elite intellectuals and politicians have assumed. It is instead, they insist, to be at the vanguard of a global popular repudiation of the neoliberal economic model that delivers wealth for the few and misery for the majority.

These cultural activists, who John Beverley might consider "organic intellectuals of the subaltern" (1999, 14), challenge fossilized indigenista notions that equate indigeneity with non-modernity. Indigenous activists insist that they will not be dissolved into a state structure and national cultural identity that does not recognize the indigenous as such, but instead, will take the lead in creating what the Zapatistas call "a world in which many worlds may fit."

These indigenous intellectuals must contend with stereotypical representations of indigenous peoples in films and televisions shows. Here, indigenous characters played by white actors imitate broken Spanish while gingerly stepping through the woods wearing white *catres* and black *rebozos*. In the following chapters we shall see that in murals and novels indigenous peoples are portrayed as one-dimensional cultural icons with stony faces and downcast eyes, victims of a social disease whose cure is assimilation to a bread-eating, knife-and-fork using, shoe-wearing, concrete-floor–dwelling mestizo ideal.

Indigenismo has been enmeshed in the process of national popular state consolidation in Mexico from roughly the 1940s to the 1970s. Hence, while it draws a parallel between indigeneity and marginalization, it stops short of critiquing the ruling party state's role in perpetuating that marginalization. Instead, indigenista theorists and administrators focus animosity on the surviving remnants of both pre-revolutionary oligarchies and indigenous communities themselves. These representations underscore intellectuals' persistent role as mediators between an overly paternalistic and repressive state and a population at once edified and excluded by that state.

In the chapters that follow, we will be able to note how this mediation has shifted ground, in the sense that acculturation is no longer unidirectional. Today, non-indigenous intellectuals often seek to channel the emergence of indigenous voices speaking against the state and its interests and to redefine what indigeneity means in the wider Mexican cultural imagination. These changes are linked to the ways in which previously held notions of intellectual property and the individual author/historical subject are being challenged by new communications technologies and new strategies of political resistance.

Indigenismo was absorbed into the state in the 1940s and began to founder in the 1960s and 1970s. Some indigenista intellectuals have functioned as brokers and beneficiaries of state hegemony; others have been renegade figures trying to dismantle official indigenista ideology and practice from within state academic, social, and cultural institutions. In the chapters that follow, I will continue to look at the mediated expressions of indigenous life and thought in Mexico, seeing how that mediation is being recast both from within and from outside indigenous communities in Mexico.

Narrating the Indian as Other

Foundational Indigenista Fictions

Indigenistas are obsessed with the indigenous as *other*. Improvising the role of cultural interpreters, they cast indigenous peoples as spiritually central yet socially peripheral to the nation. Indigenismo anchors nationalist sentiment in ideals of pre-conquest valor and dignity, yet considers living indigenous peoples as dependents rather than protagonists of the nation. By defining indigeneity in terms of lack, in terms of measurable distance from both past civilization and modern present, indigenismo negates the possibility that indigenous peoples have their own historical project. It obscures the fact that Indians and mestizos of today are the direct heirs to one of the world's most complex and sophisticated civilizations.[1] This epistemic violence echoes and enables the myriad forms of abuse of indigenous peoples in Mexican society.

As we saw in chapter one, Octavio Paz's inert and passive "Indian" bears little relation to the peoples it presumes to illuminate. As a studied simulacrum,[2] Paz's formulation has taken on a life of its own, effacing indigenous subjectivity and shaping government policies that have directly affected indigenous peoples' well-being.

Yet art seldom reflects or is implicated in political ideologies and power structures in straightforward ways. In this chapter, I examine three classic indigenista novels, *El indio* (1935), by Gregorio López y Fuentes, *El resplandor* (1937), by Mauricio Magdaleno, and *Lola Casanova* (1943), by Francisco Rojas González. At first glance, these novels appear to support state-sponsored planned acculturation projects and inspire their readers to get involved in solving "the Indian problem." A deeper look, however, reveals something more troubling about official or state-sponsored indigenismo's "political unconscious," to borrow Fredric Jameson's key term (1981). On one hand, these novels reveal middle and upper class anxieties toward bringing indigenous peoples into the mainstream of Mexican society as equals; on the other, they reveal the post-revolutionary elites' pursuit of rural capitalist development under the benevolent guise of revolutionary social justice for indigenous peasants.

As we have seen in the previous chapter, indigenismo is, among other things, a social welfare policy grounded in the academic discipline of applied anthropology. Its mission has been to integrate indigenous groups into the mainstream of Spanish-speaking national cultural and economic life. Yet indigenista action has also served to extend political and economic control into the farthest reaches of the national territory, mapping out regional networks in which to insert representatives of the ruling party as brokers and beneficiaries of agricultural production and natural resource extraction. It is this second, latent aim of indigenismo, only indirectly alluded to in official discourse, that surfaces in these novels.

Vicarious Participant Observation

As a literary practice, I consider indigenismo as the fictionalization of indigenous communal life and consciousness by non-indigenous writers. Indigenista narratives are produced and consumed within a predominantly Spanish-speaking white and mestizo cultural milieu. They are characterized by two thematic features: first, sympathy with indigenous peoples' struggles against colonial and neocolonial oppression; and second, a representational mode akin to that of an amateur ethnographer. The indigenista narrator fictionalizes the psychological, spiritual, and cultural dynamics of indigenous communities, creating an exaggerated portrait of those aspects that make the indigenous characters seem alien to the non-indigenous reader. In these texts, the narrator acts as an interpreter, introducing the reader to a fictional community through a familiar cognitive frame (usually a novel or short story) that serves as a window onto an otherwise mysterious and elusive cultural reality. The reader, in the act of consuming indigenista fiction, virtually accompanies the pseudo-ethnographer across a threshold, swept up like a vicarious participant observer on a fictional fieldwork expedition.

My initial characterization of *El indio, El resplandor,* and *Lola Casanova* as foundational indigenista novels draws its inspiration from Doris Sommer's well-known theory of "the metonymic association between romantic love that needs the state's blessing and political legitimacy that needs to be founded on love" in nineteenth-century Latin American literature (41). In *Foundational Fictions*, Sommer explains that these narratives reflect the intimate relationship between literary production and bourgeois state formation in Latin America. Foundational fictions, she argues, rest on the assumption that "literature has the capacity to intervene in history, to help construct it" (1991, 10). Quoting Pascal, Sommer notes: "Content to construct personal and public discourses 'upon each other without end' . . . foundational novels are precisely those fictions that try to pass for truth and to become the ground for political association" (1991, 45). She considers foundational literary texts as those in which individual lovelorn characters function as metonyms for whole sectors of society. In turn, the literary plots in which the characters move about function as allegories of national consolidation through erotic alliances between ethnically, economically, or politically heterogeneous social agents.

Sommer's theory of nineteenth-century foundational fictions helps us to understand how indigenista novels of the 1930s and 1940s mirror the concurrent development of indigenista social policies. The difference I note here is that in Mexican indigenista novels, the characters who broker such social alliances between heterogeneous sectors of society, those who "construct personal and public discourses upon each other without end," are more likely to be rural schoolteachers or cultural missionaries of the state than the Indian and Criollo consorts of nineteenth-century romantic *indianista* literature. Yet what makes *foundational* an apt term for these twentieth-century texts is that they too "try to pass for truth and to become the ground for political association."

Agrarian modernization, rural education, and social reconciliation through mestizaje are all prevalent themes in indigenista novels. Points of ideological ambivalence are reflected in sudden reversals of plot and character development. This becomes especially clear in the depiction of a stock character in indigenista novels, the rural schoolteacher. This character functions as intermediary between indigenous and non-indigenous communities, brokering or failing to broker alliances between them. This schoolteacher's intentions to bring "modernity and social justice" to the farthest corners of the nation are easily cast aside and personal ambitions lead to his or her corruption and cooptation by local elites. Through this ambivalent character, the narrator expresses ambivalent attitudes toward the post-revolutionary state that we do not find in official indigenista discourse.

These indigenista novels are influenced by socialist realism, naturalism, and romanticism, as well as other genres in vogue in Latin American and Spanish literary production, such as *costumbrismo* and *tremendismo*.[4] As a character, "the Indian" is constructed as a collective singular entity, a hermetic being identifiable from outside by markers of radical cultural and ethnic difference, such as dress, food preparation, and spiritual practices. If the narration is convincing, the reader develops a cozy armchair traveler's illusion of familiarity with the life of a particular indigenous group as the plot progresses.

Blending literary and social scientific narrative conventions, these novels are peppered with authorial essay, wherein the author interrupts the narrator to explain and evaluate the characters' motives and actions in terms of real or supposed cultural difference. This creates an unconscious pact between narrator and reader whereby indigenous subjectivity is overlooked.

Gregorio López y Fuentes's *El indio* (1935) is a key foundational indigenista text. The story takes place in a remote mountain village in López y Fuentes's native state of Veracruz. Although it is situated in a moment contemporary with the novel's publication, the first two thirds function as an allegory of conquest, a Manichean dramatization of the brutality of the white man toward the Indian.[5] At every turn, representations of this brutality, coupled with representations of the indigenous characters' frustrated attempts to resist this domination, create an ambivalent tone of strident denunciation and mournful resignation.

The novel opens with the brusque arrival of three white men demanding gold and medicinal plants. From that initial encounter, the previously harmonious village enters an inexorable cycle of degradation and penury. Two related events unleash this destruction: in the first chapter, "Mestizaje," one of the white explorers rapes an Indian woman. Then, the young man who was soon to marry her is chosen by the village elders to guide the explorers. Ostensibly, he is to aid them in their search for gold, but in fact, is instructed to exhaust and disorient them in the mountainous jungle. At this point, the narrator's fascination with the young Indian woman's beauty shifts to focus on the young man's physique, contemplated as if from the vantage point of the gold-seekers traipsing behind him: "given his height, his grace and his air of dignity, he was a noble vestige of a race that had once been great and strong" (45). The narrator describes the protagonist's physical characteristics with a sensual, voyeuristic delight. His physical prowess is contrasted with the ineptness and fatigue of the white explorers:

> While the white men stopped to observe a plant that had caught their attention as they penetrated the dense foliage, their guide rid himself of his shirt, tying it to his waist. When they resumed their climb,

those behind him could not help but admire the man: a body more
svelte than strong. Nothing of the bulky musculature of athletes. But
what stamina in the hike and at work! When he seized the machete to
strike a blow, his forearm showed its sinuous grace. Copper polished
by sun and labor. Statue in motion, carved of new cedar. (47–48)

Here, an erotic investment in the possession of indigenous labor and fertile or resource-rich land is transposed onto the protagonist's body itself,
which is likened to polished copper and to a young cedar tree. Aside from
the visual pleasure he affords, he is being sized up by the narrator for his
potential as a laborer. In a later passage the villagers are likened to obedi-
ent ants as they work together in the energetic building of a road. This
reinforces the novel's unconscious indigenista drive.

When the men become impatient with the young guide's silence as to
the whereabouts of the gold they seek, they throw him from a cliff, leaving
him for dead. At this point, the narrator's obsession with the Indian's powerful physique turns to preoccupation with his physical and psychological
disfiguration after his fall. This character, henceforth identified simply as
"the cripple" (el lisiado), functions as a metonym for the narrator's vision of
present-day indigenous peoples, who were once "great and strong" but are
now deemed "invalids." The following passage detailing the guide's misfortune illustrates the narrator's pity:

The couples waited their turn for their wedding ceremony. The cripple, half hidden behind a rocky ledge, could not take his eyes off one
of the couples. . . . He gaped at them from far off, with a sorrow as
immense as the apparent indifference of his race. . . . Already certain
of the outcome of the scene about to take place before the priest, he
set out for his home, steadying himself on his crude crutch before the
couple might approach. His left leg, completely disfigured, gave him
the appearance of someone about to kneel down, as his thigh almost
touched his ankle, and that was the good leg, the one that held up
his body; the other leg, twisted in front, made a circular motion each
time he lurched forward. (47)

As this passage suggests, the protagonist has lost his intended bride to
another man because his disfigurement has caused him to become "inválido"
(an invalid but also, impotent), unleashing a family feud that will erode the
community as the novel progresses. The young bride, having been raped
at the outset of the novel by the gold-seekers, disappears from the plot at
this point. Much like La Malinche in the nationalist myth, her importance
here is as a catalyst for actions among men; since the misfortunes suffered

by her community began when she was raped, her social function is that of scapegoat (see chap. 5).

The first two parts of the novel are allegorical, depicting time as cyclical and fluid, a relentless reenactment of the Conquest. The final third, however, situates the mountain village in the context of 1930s Mexico. Caught between the opposing powers of Church, state, and landowners who refuse to cede their traditional dominance, the indigenous villagers struggle to appease all three. These factions compete for the allegiance and labor of the villagers, who then find no time or energy to tend their *milpas* (small plots of land for individual, family, and community sustenance) and are faced with increasing misery, compounded by a smallpox epidemic.

First, the government enlists their labor to build a road and a school, neither of which actually helps them: the road circumvents their hamlet, and the rural schoolteacher leaves, unable and unwilling to communicate with his Nahuatl-speaking pupils and disgusted with the "ignorance of the natives" (151). Competing with the government, the priest convinces the villagers to build a church and make a pilgrimage to the shrine of a nearby saint in gratitude for sparing them from the smallpox epidemic and famine that have ravaged their village.

The novel's climax is precipitated by the arrival of a second schoolteacher, this time an upstart native of a nearby village. This indigenous character represents the acculturated Indian, who interprets government authority and modern mestizo values for the non-acculturated indigenous characters. At first, he appears to be the community's heroic advocate who will ensure that land reform and new labor laws are enforced. His connections with the federal government, his education in the capital, his knowledge of the law, as well as his intimate relationship to the language and struggles of the villagers allow him to act as a mediator, bringing the indigenous people into active political participation. When the schoolteacher begins his work, he is appalled by the poverty and abuses of authority to which the villagers are subjected. He is horrified to see that conditions are as if the Revolution had not touched his region. As this passage indicates, the schoolteacher becomes the village's leader, resolving to bring the benefits of revolutionary justice to the people:

> The schoolteacher, upon organizing his lesson plans, realized that he must make a social commitment [to the community] as well. His brothers confessed to him that they were still obliged to perform free labor, even though it had been legally abolished: He had to denounce this abuse, even if it brought the animosity of town authorities upon him. . . . He explained the nature of the new laws as well as he could.

And to convince them, he told them that the most important government leaders were about to save all the peasants, especially the Indians, thanks to their schools and their economic programs, such as land distribution. (154–155)

Yet the schoolteacher undergoes a sudden transformation in motivation and personality. His sincere desire for justice quickly gives way to personal ambition as his charismatic political agitation gains him favor among local politicians. Eager to gain popular support, the schoolteacher-turned-political-agitator cynically convinces the villagers to take land reform into their own hands; he distributes guns among them so that they may confront the mercenary white guards who protect the landowners' usurped holdings. Once his own position is assured, the schoolteacher abruptly leaves the village to take a job "in the city." The villagers are left worse off than ever at the novel's end, having to defend themselves against the constant attacks of the white guards. "The cripple" reappears as the emblematic Indian of indigenista novels, suspicious and distrustful of outsiders. The schoolteacher, however, is depicted as the emblematic acculturated Indian, selling his own people down the river for personal gain.

> The cripple keeps watch, crouching in his hiding place, distrust gazing out at the road—the road that is civilization—from his trench. From high up in the mountains, another waits for the signal. As with all of his kind, they only know that the "people of reason" (*gente de razón*) want to attack them; that in the hills and in the valley, their hatred, their lynch-dogs bare their teeth; and that their leader is well-off and comfortable in the city. (164)

With the leader's arrival, we had been led to consider that the narrator was endorsing bilingual education and land reform. That position is later retracted, however, as the schoolteacher suddenly betrays the causes and the people he had so vehemently supported. At first, the narrator appears to endorse the entrance of indigenous groups into regional and national political processes; ultimately, however, he plunges the characters into a cycle of repression, thus revealing a deeper fear of the ultimate consequences of radical change in the social structure. At the novel's end, the indigenous villagers are in worse shape for having broken out of their isolation. The government has offered them hope of modifying deep-seated caste relations but is ultimately unable or unwilling to deliver on that promise. Indigenismo is as necessary as it is doomed.

Mauricio Magdaleno's 1937 novel *El resplandor* shows us an equally pessimistic view of the post-revolutionary state's ability to include indigenous peoples in its programs for social justice and modernization. Magdaleno depicts the revolutionary gains, especially those of rural education and land reform, as frustrated by the greed and corruption of local warlords (*caciques*). In this novel, a landless Otomí (*ñañhu*) village in the Valle del Mesquital in the State of Hidalgo is the perpetual victim of white and mestizo trickery. Saturnino Herrera, a mestizo orphan raised at the breast of an Otomí woman, Lugarda, is the novel's malevolent antagonist. The collective protagonist is the Otomí village of San Andrés de la Cal, bound in servitude to the hacienda La Brisa. When the young Herrera is sent away to boarding school in the nearby city of Pachuca as part of a government program to stimulate rural education, the *tlacuaches* (possums, the narrator's derogatory pet name for the Otomíes) hope their prodigal son will one day return to defend them from the landowners' abuses. When he returns as governor of Hidalgo, he fills them with false promises of good land and protection from greedy landlords. All the while, he grows rich on their labor. Having married the heiress of La Brisa, he is now their master disguised as their savior.

Saturnino Herrera is mestizo, but he is not the archetypal "son of la Malinche" born of a Spanish father and an indigenous mother described in chapter five. A product of the rape of a white woman by a plundering indigenous revolutionary, Herrera is mestizo on his way to becoming white. Through his son, born of his fair-skinned and aristocratic wife Matilde, his paternal indigenous origins can be hidden. He admits to being the adopted son of Lugarda, but he insists that *his son* bears no trace of indigenous ancestry or sensibility. He states, "I was an Indian, almost, and Rafaelito is the son of Matilde" (117).

Through his son, Herrera has broken away from his indigenous roots, denying his own father just as his son will have to deny *him* in order to be considered white. But Herrera's other, nameless son is the child that will be born at the novel's end to Lorenza, the Otomí woman whom he raped upon his arrival to San Andrés de la Cal as a gubernatorial candidate. As in *El indio*, the young indigenous woman is central to the novel's plot, but only as a catalyst for the action involving the struggle for land and influence that later unfolds between men. After she is raped, Lorenza is no longer a central character, but one whose reproductive cycle silently marks the relentless passage of time after conquest. The fate of the newborn bastard is left to the reader's imagination. Will he become another nameless *tlacuache*, an "*hijo de la Chingada*" as Paz would have it, doomed to relive the same cycles of subjugation suffered by his mother and grandmother? Or will he, like his father, leave San Andrés and return one day to betray the people that raised him? Either way, as the novel closes with the newborn's mournful birth-cry and the kidnapping of another Otomí child to be schooled in Pachuca, the narrator offers the fatalistic conclusion that both the infant and the school-bound boy will be limited by the same caste relations into which they were born. Their roles in the village will be to renew the cycles of hope and disappointment that have marked the novel's rhythm throughout.

Though they know he has raped Lorenza, and they see that his promises of land and an irrigation system never materialize, the Otomí villagers' adulation of Herrera is slow to dissolve. They are left to starve while the fruits of their labor, jealously guarded by Herrera's cruel administrator, Felipe Rendón, fill the granaries and are trucked out to market. The villagers refer to Rendón as "the executioner" after he lynches three hungry villagers who tried to steal some corn. At the novel's climax, the villagers kill Rendón in a famished rage as they see the last of the harvest leave the hacienda. His murder unleashes a harrowing revenge by Rendón's brother, who lynches eight of the village leaders, including Bonifacio, who, as his name suggests, had been the last to give up hope on Herrera's benevolence. Bonifacio's interior monologue reveals the narrator's pessimism about the fate of this calcified village, which is repeatedly described as Hell, abandoned by the priest, by God, and even by San Andrés, the village's patron saint.

As he heads out of town, Rendón's brother sets the villagers' straw and adobe homes ablaze, simply to crown his revenge. In the wake of this destruction, the Otomí villagers are reluctant to work at La Brisa. But starvation eventually brings them back to tend Saturnino Herrera's thriving fields, dairies, and distilleries once again.

The new administrator tries in vain to win back their loyalty to Herrera's empire by building a school and contracting a schoolteacher. It is too late, however; although the idealistic teacher would like to help them fight Herrera and his cronies' abuses, the villagers are convinced he has been sent by their enemy, and that the school is just another means of controlling them. As in *El indio*, the narrator expresses an ambivalent though ultimately fatalistic vision of rural education and the ability of the state to act on behalf of indigenous peasants. At the novel's end, the villagers watch helplessly as government representatives sequester the schoolteacher's brightest pupil who, like Herrera a generation before, is to be educated in Pachuca. Thus, as with *El indio*, the novel concludes that education for indigenous peoples is a force that compounds rather than ameliorates their problems.

Rather than the romantic intrigues between interethnic lovers characteristic of nineteenth-century Latin American novels, these foundational indigenista novels feature metonymic associations between dark, fertile soil and the wombs and (milk-producing) breasts of indigenous female characters. The persistence of this metaphor in these texts suggests something akin to what Sommer describes as an "interlocking, not parallel, relationship between erotics and politics" (43). Thus, the narrator of *El resplandor* describes the earth in a freshly tilled field as "dark like the womb of an Indian woman" (64). In these novels, indigenous women are characterized solely in terms of their reproductive and life-sustaining capacities, as victims of rape, bearers of children conceived through rape, and bearers of breast milk destined to give life not to their own babies but to the children of land-owning whites. In *El diosero*, Francisco Rojas González derides the crassness with which a white couple in search of a wetnurse for their baby reduces one nursing Indian woman to her breasts, which the narrator describes as "beautiful brown-skinned breasts, tremulous as a pair of udders ready to burst" (Rojas González, 1952, 29). In all of these novels, indigenous female characters function as reproductive vessels and catalysts for plot development.[5]

This narrative transposition between eroticized indigenous women's bodies (or laboring indigenous men's bodies, as we saw in the case of *El indio*) and agriculturally or ore-rich land is the key to understanding how indigenista literature reflects the political unconscious of indigenista social policies. Foundational indigenista novels such as these (and, as we shall see in a moment, *Lola Casanova*) share a libidinal investment in making fictional inroads into the agriculturally productive countryside and in constructing strategic alliances between the consuming capital city and the countryside. This fantasy of possession of the countryside and its agricultural bounty is allegorized in the violent, dehumanizing possession by white male characters of indigenous female characters' bodies, which are often described by the narrators as fertile earth, as rounded earthen pottery, or as milk-producing cows. Clearly, beyond the white and mestizo male characters' twisted drive to subjugate and dehumanize indigenous women, there is also a narrative drive to capture and domesticate the life-sustaining potential these bodies are made to represent. The accelerated internal colonization of the countryside is thus transposed, in literary discourse, onto fictionalized indigenous women's bodies. These bodies are depicted as the site of struggle between antagonistic sectors of society, namely the surviving remnants of the Porfirian rural oligarchy and the newly hegemonic national bourgeoisie.

Francisco Rojas González's *Lola Casanova* (1947) provides an important counterpoint to the two novels outlined above. It occupies a peculiar place within the Mexican indigenista genre, as it mimics the interethnic romances of nineteenth century indianismo, yet ironically proves to be more focused upon validating the official twentieth century indigenista project of ethnic assimilation and agro-industrial modernization. Whereas the novels discussed above pair negative consequences with mestizaje—rape, betrayal, and degradation—here mestizaje functions much like in official indigenista discourse, as the only viable path to social reconciliation. Tinged with nineteenth-century romanticism and the racy stuff of dime-store novels, *Lola Casanova* tells the story of the beautiful and charming daughter of a Catalán businessman. Lola is captured and captivated by a godlike Seri (Yaqui) warrior, constantly described by the narrator as "Herculean." The initial conflict, in which Lola is taken prisoner, immediately presents itself as the solution that allows her to escape a dreaded marriage alliance between herself and a rapacious and arrogant killer of Yaquis. Within a short time, Lola falls in love with her Seri warrior captor, bears several children with him, and becomes acculturated into his nomadic group. Her acculturation is achieved through a series of rituals in which she proves her loyalty to her new community. These rituals culminate in the marriage ceremony between herself and her beloved warrior, where she dons the traditional dress made of pelican feathers and shells and sheds her Christian name for that of Iguana (209).

Her integration brings many changes for the Seris as well. She gains the respect of those in her new community by instructing them in modern hygiene, farming, and craft-making techniques. She convinces them to cease their nomadic hunting and gathering and take up a sedentary life, trading their handicrafts and agricultural products with the mestizos. In this sense, the novel enacts a wish fulfillment in keeping with the INI's ideological imperatives. Just as the anthropologist working for the INI aimed to gain the favor of the most powerful and respected members of a community in order to persuade them to cooperate with government initiatives, Lola's acculturation to Seri life is actually a mechanism for the assimilation of the Seris to national culture. She functions as a cultural missionary, subtly suppressing the "negative" aspects of Seri culture and bringing out the "useful" ones. Thus Lola has managed to infiltrate the community and influence its leaders to adapt to national models of economic and social development. In passages that read like pamphlets produced by the Fondo Nacional para las Artes (FONART) or the Fondo Nacional para el Turismo (FONATUR), the narrator celebrates the fact that, through their production of *artesanías* and their transformation of a patch of desert into an agricultural oasis, the Seris cease to be "savages" and become exemplary mestizos:

They live now with the exaltation of endless work. In their homes, meztizo industry flourishes in all its forms and accomplishments. From women's hands come weavings of reeds and grasses, famous for being so tightly woven that not even a drop of liquid seeps between their fibers; wooden boxes delicately encrusted with shells; light and flexible hats and bags made of aromatic palm leaves. . . . Commerce is also mestizo: produced and sold by *yoreme* [Seri], consumed by *yori* [white].

But the Seris of Pozo Coyote are also laborers, as lands ripped from the sterility of the plain now fill with lush foliage.

Water, extracted from wells by animal labor or by the might of men's muscles, runs its fingers through canals and streams, leaving in its wake a breadbasket. . . . But this agriculture is mestizo, too: the work is done by Seris; but the fruit of the land, oh noble grandmother! goes to the white man, indefatigable entrepreneur. (267)

In contrast, a renegade Seri faction, which does not become sedentary but continues to wander and wage war against the "yoris" (mestizos and whites) is described as having fallen prey to social disintegration, drunkenness, promiscuity, and sloth. The key to the "good" Seris' successful integration into national society resides in their having relinquished all "negative" cultural traits, such as warfare, hunting, the eating of raw meat, and having learned to exaggerate and profit from some of their more "positive" cultural particularities to appeal to mestizo and white consumers. While the narrator chastises the "bad" Seris for following the "putrid tradition" (268), he rejoices in the productive alliance between "la criolla" and the Indian chief, "now transformed into an enthusiastic captain of industry" (242):

Commerce, noble medium of the relations between peoples, is born in Bahía Kino under the influence of the criolla's will. . . . But it's necessary to make sure it follows a rational path: the exchange of pearls for trinkets makes for a ruinous exchange. . . . Iguana improves the technique and refines the taste of the new basketmaking entrepreneurs. . . . Fishing is intensified and enthusiasm for gathering grows: each family's hut is now a warehouse or a workshop, and from them come items for exchange which are received with pleasure by the middlemen, now transformed into feverish participants and defenders of peace with the Seri people. (241–42)

What sets *Lola Casanova* apart from the other foundational indigenista novels discussed above is its optimism. The successful transformation of the Seris, under the tutelage of Lola Casanova, is offered as proof that the precepts of official indigenismo can be successfully applied to effect cultural change in indigenous communities, even in those whose traditional practices are deemed most radically opposite to those of national culture.

These indigenista literary representations have served to legitimize official indigenista discourses and policies that were being elaborated during this same time period. In indigenista literature and policy, "Indian" is equated with "landless peasant" but also with "malleable." In this sense, these novels have played a fundamental, albeit indirect role in the shaping of a hegemonic vision of indigeneity as something that must be explained, transformed, or expiated in order for Mexico to achieve that elusive and desired condition called modernity. Yet cultural production—whether in the form of art, novels, or poetry—always contains multiple and conflicting impulses, so even the most seemingly hegemonic of texts can be read for the ways in which they betray counter-hegemonic impulses within them.

In all three of these novels, the urban middle and upper classes— which create and consume indigenista fiction—are consistently placed on a moral high ground, written out of the script, exonerated so that they can be the privileged disseminator and audience of this literature. As in official indigenista discourse, multiple layers of exploitation born of urban- rural and transnational capitalism are drastically oversimplified in order to stage an epic struggle between white landowners and Indians. The literary and political discourses elaborated around indigenous peoples' existence address cosmopolitan middle-class readers, certainly not the villainous white landholders or the exploited illiterate indigenous peasants these novels portray. The indigenista literary project, then, is at an impasse: On one hand, it cannot radically alter dominant stereotypes of the indigenous as *other*, because the absence of the referent leads to the projection of non- Indian cognitive and aesthetic imperatives onto its fictionalized indigenous landscapes. On the other hand, literary indigenismo represents indigenous people not as engaged in an ongoing resistance to European and Creole colonization, but as pawns in the struggle between the semi-feudal oli- garchy and the emerging national bourgeoisie, whose hegemony-making strategy has placed a premium on the modernization and homogenization of national culture and thus the subordination of local forms of identifica- tion and local subsistence economies.

In these foundational indigenista narratives, as in official indigenismo, supposedly intrinsic cultural factors determine the indigenous subjects' poverty and exploitation, rather than the historical weight of imperialism and racist inequality. So, although they may condemn Mexican society as a whole for its indifference to the marginalization of "its" indigenous populations, they ultimately condemn indigenous peoples themselves for being unable to rise above these supposed cultural limitations to which they stubbornly cling.

These novels bolster the hegemonic indigenista ideology that casts the present-day Indian as a passive object of pity and lament. They posit an unstable and vexing solution to the problem of indigenous marginalization within the imperatives of national modernization and progress: While the first two novels that were discussed fatalistically conclude that indigenous peoples are unredeemable, fated to die by government-sanctioned violence against them rather than be incorporated into the nation, the last holds out a cynical promise that incorporation into capitalist production on the lowest rung of the ladder will bring the only possible redemption. By contrast, the characters that struggle to maintain their unfettered way of life are punished with alcoholism, starvation, and oblivion. Thus, the overwhelming sense of impotence and resignation attributed to these novels' indigenous characters is not only the product of racist prejudice. It is also a projection of the narrators' own sense of futility when confronted with the incommensurability of revolutionary struggle and institutionalized revolution.

Each of the foundational indigenista novels discussed here constructs an imploded universe of economic and moral exploitation. The goal is not so much to create an identification of the reader with the indigenous characters, but to bring the reader to despise the white landowners and to conclude that intervention from outside mediators is necessary in order to transform both the indigenous and the white or mestizo elements. That this outside mediation has little or nothing to do with land reform and everything to do with fixing cultures is part and parcel of the indigenista imperatives that inform these novels' plot structures, imagery, and character development.

3

The Ethnographic Coming-of-age Story

Three mid-twentieth-century indigenista literary and ethnographic texts, *Juan Pérez Jolote* (1952), by Ricardo Pozas, *Los hombres verdaderos* (*The True Peoples*, 1959), by Carlo Antonio Castro, and *Oficio de tinieblas* (*The Book of Lamentations*, 1962), by Rosario Castellanos, reflect the changing construction of indigeneity in the Mexican cultural imagination as the PRI further institutionalized indigenismo in the latter half of the twentieth century. These narratives blend literary and ethnographic elements, telling the story of an urban intelligentsia coming to terms with the ethno-linguistic heterogeneity of the nation. In contrast with their foundational predecessors, however, they break out of the omniscient narrative point of view we find in previous ethnographic and literary works, adopting instead the first person singular point of view of their indigenous informants and protagonists. Nevertheless, particularly in the case of the first two texts, determining the extent to which these perspectives are filtered and recast by their non-indigenous authors is an elusive goal. Though mediated through the explicit indigenista prerogatives of their authors, these texts give us a sense of how indigenous peoples have coped with the government's attempts to incorporate them into a new agrarian order under a highly centralized and authoritarian state. To the extent that they represent indigenous peoples as agents within the nation, they anticipate the development of the testimonial genre that emerged in full force in the 1980s and 1990s (see chap. 4).

These proto-testimonial texts interpret the countryside and its indigenous inhabitants for an urban readership. They reflect a newfound awareness among urban elites of the existence of this rural and ethnically heterogeneous reality. This awareness is not mere curiosity: the hegemony of the emergent national bourgeoisie depends directly on knowing and controlling the countryside and its inhabitants. Through its indigenista programs, the ruling party used the memory of the Revolution and its promise of social justice as a doorway to that countryside.

At the time these texts were published, the PRI had become adept at invoking the Revolution as a shared event in the life of the nation and as perpetual promise, safeguarded and carried into the future by its very institutionalization. At the same time, spurred on in part by the United States' production demands during the Second World War, the government began to reorient its economy toward securing foreign investment and expanding the country's industrial and agricultural capacities. High population growth and significant rural-to-urban migration created a labor force for this growth.[1]

The increase in internal migration was driven by a rise in wages for urban workers as well as stagnation in land redistribution after 1940.[2] While President Cárdenas (1934–1940) had distributed 44 million acres, his successor, President Ávila Camacho (1940–1946) distributed only about 11 million (Skidmore and Smith, 2001, 238). In order to increase the national food supply and promote industrial development, Presidents Ávila Camacho and, after him, Miguel Alemán (1946–1952) focused on allocating land to individual families, rather than to the communally owned *ejidos* based on traditional indigenous patterns of land ownership that had been favored by Cárdenas (Fehrenbach, 1995, 607). With this reversal of agrarian policy, ideas about the place of indigenous peoples within the nation changed as well.

In this era of infrastructural development (roads, dams, communications, port facilities, irrigation, and hydroelectric projects), local and national economic networks became increasingly intertwined. While these public works facilitated industrial and export-oriented agribusiness development in the north, the central *meseta* and mountainous southern and southeastern states became the focus of small-scale agricultural production for regional and national consumption. Just as many peasants left the countryside to join the ranks of the urban proletariat in Mexico City, many urbanites representing a new class of technocrats, bureaucrats, and entrepreneurs who were associated with the PRI ventured out of the capital with ambitious plans to extend their political and economic reach throughout the country.

The PRI was redirecting Cárdenas' socialist agrarian and educational policies toward the aims of national integration and capitalist accumulation. The earlier indigenista formulation of the Indian as hermetic and alien to modernity was no longer politically expedient. INI specialists sought instead to measure indigenous assimilation to national culture, language, and socioeconomic life. With improved communication and circulation of people and ideas between Mexico City and outlying regions, their formulation of indigeneity shifted from that of a spatially and temporally remote archetype to that of a stubborn reminder of the uneven modernity Mexico had yet to overcome.

Ethnographic, pedagogic, and development work carried out within the INI's regional coordinating centers was oriented toward integrating indigenous communities to the national system. The development of the INI's rural infrastructure fed into this larger process of drawing on the agriculturally productive countryside and its inhabitants to facilitate industrial and agricultural development—a process that depended on the creation of a labor force induced to abandon subsistence agriculture and local forms of identification and collective association.

Ethnography as Literature

At mid-twentieth century, a shift in the conventions of ethnographic writing reflects changes in fieldwork methods. As portable tape-recording devices became a mainstay of fieldwork, informants' perspectives began to take center stage in ethnographic writing. Oscar Lewis brought the new fieldwork methods of participant observation and tape-recording of informants' voices into his chronicles of inner-city poverty in Mexico City in widely read works such as *Five Families* (1959) and *Children of Sánchez* (1961), bringing literary conventions into social scientific writing. Like Lewis, Ricardo Pozas and Carlo Antonio Castro brought the voices of their indigenous informants into their ethnographic works, creating texts that read as individual bildungsroman or coming-of-age stories. In turn, cultural relativism and participant observation changed the way these ethnographers approached cultural differences, humanizing their research and bringing them to question the indigenista ideal of a homogeneous mestizo society.

Cynthia Hewitt de Alcántara (1984) explains the mid-twentieth century waning of the functionalist paradigm, which had dominated anthropological discourse throughout the 1920s, 30s, and much of the 40s, in terms of this intensified contact between country and city. The functionalist paradigm had considered indigenous peasant communities to exist in a temporal and spatial vacuum; just as the object of study (the folk community) was to be apprehended as a closed system, the anthropologist was to analyze that system from a position deemed absolutely exterior to it. According to Hewitt, this paradigm was undermined when during the 1950s, a growing number of anthropologists working in Mexico stepped outside the geographical confines of the isolated rural community and the temporal confines of the functionalist present. They began to see not so much what separated rural people from the wider socioeconomic system as what integrated them; not so much the characteristic features of disparity as those of domination. That this turn of events was intimately related to the changing nature of life in the Mexican countryside could hardly be denied: in Mexico as in most of the rest of the world, rural areas were rapidly being integrated into new kinds of socioeconomic and political arrangements congruent with the development of modernizing nation states. (42)

This change from a functionalist to a structuralist and later, post-structuralist orientation would eventually open the door to a radical questioning of indigenismo as epistemology and as social practice. These new methods of fieldwork involved living for extended periods among indigenous groups and adapting to everyday life within these communities. In the long run, by positing a non-hierarchical relationship between cultures and making room for indigenous perspectives, these new models of intercultural and interclass communication eventually provided indigenous peoples with the means through which to express their own subjectivity and notions of national belonging.

This genre that I am calling the ethnographic coming-of-age story breaks from traditional ethnographic writing practices by transferring the authorial voice to indigenous informants, whose orally related first-person accounts are transcribed and reorganized by the ethnographer. Hence, the ethnographer appears to the reader as more of a conduit or interlocutor than an omniscient describer of a reality outside him- or herself. *Juan Pérez Jolote* and *Los hombres verdaderos* introduce the reader to the customs and worldview of a given community through the perspective of individual informants. The ethnographer tells us that the informants are metonyms; through their tales, the reader is invited to view a microcosm of the community as a whole.

These narratives feature indigenous characters that venture out of the confines of their villages to interact within wider social milieus. In this sense, the characters represent the acculturation process through which indigenous communities selectively adapt and transform elements of the national culture into their own village life. In these texts, previously fixed notions of author and protagonist, of subject and object become dislodged. Because they let indigenous voices dominate the texts, they no longer present a vision of indigeneity as pure simulacrum; instead, they lead the reader to conclude that indigenous life and consciousness cannot be so easily captured and controlled through indigenista action.

As these mid-twentieth century ethnographers center their writing on the first-person testimony of informants, indigenous protagonists begin to move toward center stage, offering their own perspectives on what it means to be indigenous and how they perceive being interpolated as such by non-Indian observers. With the publication of *Juan Pérez Jolote*, by Ricardo Pozas, the ethnographer's indigenista storyline of a benevolent state bringing modernization and social justice to the downtrodden indigenous is disrupted by the indigenous narrator's ambivalent vision toward that state. As we shall see, the gulf between indigenista representations of "the Indian" on one hand and indigenous self-representations on the other continues to widen as indigenous narrators are given more room to shape the narratives written about them in later testimonial texts.

A second type of indigenista narrative to emerge at this time, ethno-historical fiction, novelizes indigenous insurrections during the colonial and early independence period. Most notably, Castellanos's *Oficio de tinieblas* draws parallels between the colonial past and the post-revolutionary present in the highlands of Chiapas. It would be a mistake to think that Castellanos gets any closer to something we might call an indigenous point of view than did the novelists discussed in the previous chapter. However, what sets this novel apart from foundational indigenista fictions is that it registers the existence of class-consciousness in indigenous peoples and an awareness of the need to transform their own social conditions through struggle against local and national elites. It registers the existence of indigenous historical projects and consciousnesses that differ from those of Europeans and their descendants in Mexico. Whereas indigenismo constructs an indigenous silence, *Oficio de tinieblas* attempts to fill that silence with fictionalized indigenous protagonists of past rebellions. This novel's best feature is undoubtedly its exploration of the connection between racial and gender inequality in Mexico.

The Conflictive Heterogeneity of Indigenista Discourse

These ethnographic and ethnohistorical narratives blur traditional distinctions between the writing subject and the object of representation, between an oral-pictographic discursive field and a textual one. They are symptomatic of what Antonio Cornejo Polar considered the "conflictive heterogeneity" of indigenista literature. Some of these writers lived for extended periods among the people about whom they were writing, while others lived in nearby cities. Their relative closeness to indigenous communities allowed them to move away from earlier indigenista depictions of "the Indian" as an amorphous and mute collective singular protagonist; instead, voices of individual indigenous informants and protagonists came to occupy a central place in these transcultural narratives. Within this neo-indigenista framework, indigenous linguistic, cognitive, and civil-religious practices, as well as the ways in which indigenous informants or referents understood themselves to fit within Mexican society, are central elements of these narratives.

Based in the INI's regional coordinating centers, most notably its pilot project, the Tzotzil-Tzeltal Coordinating Center in the Chiapas highlands, this second generation of indigenista writers came to stay awhile. They dealt directly with indigenous peoples on a human level, often learning the languages spoken and observing the systems of regional domination and the social relations within the communities in which they were working. The aim of official indigenismo had been to subtly ease indigenous peoples out of their own cultures; these writers and their coming-of-age narratives profoundly altered the terms on which indigenista expertise had been established. Here, the ethnographer and fiction writer had become listener and pupil rather than detached observer and expert.

While the purpose of "applied anthropology" was to induce assimilation to the national mestizo society, language, and cultural values, that goal as prescribed by Gonzalo Aguirre Beltrán and others necessarily began with listening to and gaining the sympathy of "native informants."[3] The functionalist view of culture as static did not serve the ends of institutionally based indigenista theorists and practitioners, for whom indigenous assimilation to national mestizo culture was both necessary and inevitable. Indigenistas redefined the folk or indigenous peasant community as changeable, and the anthropologist as the primary agent in that community's transformation.

The 1952 publication of *Juan Pérez Jolote*, by Ricardo Pozas,[4] represents the first significant break from the discursive conventions of both ethnography and indigenista fiction in Mexico. It is a textual recreation of a first-person oral account of an aged man from San Juan Chamula, a Tzotzil village near the colonial city of San Cristóbal de las Casas, as told to Pozas. According to Pozas, Juan Pérez Jolote's candid reflections on his life illuminate aspects of Tzotzil culture in a more accessible way than traditional social scientific accounts.

Pozas establishes his narrative authority in the introduction, outlining the most salient features of social and economic life in San Juan Chamula and nearby villages. He justifies this change in ethnographic perspective in terms that would placate more traditional practitioners, asserting that Juan Pérez Jolote is a "typical" Chamulan man, an apt representative of his community. Pozas assures us that this man's story "should be considered a concise monograph of Chamula culture," as it contains "a clear description of the most important components of that culture" (7).

Despite the fact that it is narrated in first person, Pozas calls the text a biography. This alerts us to the fact that Pozas is not surrendering complete narrative authority to his interlocutor. Pozas has opened the door to what will become an intense questioning of the distinction between the subjectivity of the referent and that of the author in later testimonial texts. As a ghost-written autobiography related orally to an interlocutor who records, organizes, and resequences the narrative, the line between the voice of the speaker and the voice of the writer is nearly invisible to the reader, inviting speculation but no real resolution to the question of whose vision of Chamulan village life is being told.

Much like the later *Hasta no verte Jesús mío* (1969), by Elena Poniatowska, this text tells the story of a marginalized person at a dramatic juncture in national history, dislodged from his traditional community through revolutionary struggle, only to be forgotten by that nation and left to wander back into the periphery to live out the rest of his days.

Paradoxically, to be of ethnographic interest, the subject of Pozas' ethnographic "biography" must not be an acculturated indigenous person; yet he must be somewhat acculturated in order to be able to relate his life story to the anthropologist who does not speak Tzotzil. It is that partial assimilation—especially his knowledge of Spanish and his participation in the Revolution—that provides the conditions necessary for him to become the subject of Pozas's proto-testimonio. Promising a "brief monograph of Chamulan culture," he states

> Our example is typical, in that his conduct characterizes that of many men of his group (with the exception of his participation in the armed struggle of the Revolution, which was an accident in his life). His is not an exceptional biography; on the contrary, it is perfectly normal within his sphere, save the causes that brought our biographical subject to leave his village. (7)

Here, Pozas minimizes the internal conflicts (domestic violence, poverty, debt servitude, indiscriminate incarceration of indigenous people by corrupt local authorities) that brought him to abandon his village as a boy as well as the external ones (conscription of incarcerated peasants during the Revolution) that have brought him to leave the region of Chiapas as a young man, learn Spanish, and become a partially acculturated figure within his community of San Juan Chamula. Throughout the autobiographical narrative that follows, Pozas's voice disappears, hiding behind and reorganizing the narrator-protagonist's oral reflections. There are moments in which detailed descriptions of rituals and customs reveal the heavy hand of the ethnographer. For example, his descriptions of San Juan Chamula's church and its saints, the Day of the Dead ceremonies, Carnival, the cargo system, and his marriage ceremony are painstakingly narrated to be didactic, to inform the curious reader of the spiritual practices and beliefs in San Juan Chamula. In the following passage, for example, Juan Pérez Jolote describes one of the saints as follows: "This is Saint Nicholas. He is the patron saint of the hens. He carries his buckets full of corn to feed the hens. But I don't know how San Nicolás feeds the hens, since both his hands are full." (100)

Aside from these descriptions of religious life and beliefs, Juan Pérez Jolote's picaresque tales of adventure and misfortune, sexual awakening, and readjustment to life in his village turn out to be far more compelling than Pozas's dry academic description of village life in his 1959 monograph *Chamula*. The narrator begins his story by describing his childhood; he tells us that he ran away from his village to escape his brutally abusive father, only to find himself enslaved, exploited, falsely accused, and imprisoned for murder. He is set free on condition that he fight as a mercenary in a revolution he does not understand. As a narrative of the assimilation of an indigenous person to Spanish-speaking mestizo society and his eventual return to his community, it presents a negative vision of acculturation. Although he has enjoyed the prestige of taking on various "cargos" in the civil-religious hierarchy, he reckons he will drink himself to death, just as his father had before him, as the following passage suggests.

> Every day my friends come to my house. They drink with me and they come to buy [spirits]. They share with me and I drink with everyone. "Don't drink any more," my [daughters] Lorenza and Dominga say, but I can't stop drinking. I haven't eaten for days. . . . That's how my father died, but I don't want to die. I want to live. (112–113)

Like Oscar Lewis's *The Children of Sánchez* (1961), *Juan Pérez Jolote* is striking in its portrayal of chaotic brutality and patriarchal despotism within family and communal structures among marginalized groups. Both claim a social scientific objectivity and dissolve their own authorial interventions and orderings of the narrative into the texts. Unlike the later testimonios that begin to appear around the time Casa de las Américas recognized testimonio as a literary genre in 1969, these ethnographic coming-of-age stories are not explicitly presented as occasions to denounce injustices; they are instead remarkable for their shock value as tales of picaresque characters who naïvely stumble through life, never understanding the historical forces that shape them beyond the familiar spaces of neighborhood and village. They call attention to the need for social change, yet locate the agency of that change outside the indigenous communities.

In the introduction to *Los indios en las clases sociales de México* (1976), coauthored with Isabel Horcasitas de Pozas, Ricardo Pozas asserts his interest in developing a "theoretical framework for the study of the Indians as participants in national development" (4). By choosing Juan Pérez Jolote as his guide, an individual who had been away from his community for many years, Pozas breaks with the conventions of ethnographic writing established by his functionalist mentors. Whereas they had sought to understand indigenous communities as separate entities from national life, as pure islands of cultural difference, Pozas considers his informant as a symbol of national integration. He is representative of his community because his identity has been formed both within and outside of it, not in spite of that fact. For Juan Pérez Jolote, being Chamulan and belonging to his village is flexible. As the following passage suggests, when he returns after many years away, he has to relearn the language, dress, and customs:

> I came back to Chamula on August 14th, 1930; the next day was the feast day for Santa Rosa, and my father told me "the people are not going to like the way you are dressed; you'd better change." I took off my rags and they gave me a wool poncho, which I fit around me with a suede belt, over my cotton pants and shirt. Again, I was a Chamula.
> But I didn't feel comfortable with that costume; I was afraid to leave my house, I didn't want anyone to see me. I was sad and I didn't want to go to the party. . . . I was so sad; I no longer knew how to live as a Chamula. And so I thought, Why did I come back to my village? What made me come back? . . . Now everything seems so strange to me, I can't speak like my people and I have forgotten our customs. . . . I'm ashamed to dress as a Chamula, and if I dress the way I did before, I look ugly here. . . . I can't go out to the square, I think they will look down on me, and talk about me. . . .
> I stayed home, working and listening to my mother speak our language. I continued that way for many days, next to her, as if I were a child. . . . Later the feast of Rosario came and went, and I didn't go either. I didn't want people to see me dressed as a Chamula as long as I couldn't talk to them. (54–55)

Pozas does not consider Juan Pérez Jolote as exceptional for having left for many years, fighting in various factions in the Mexican Revolution, and roaming the countryside in the years following the armed struggle. Juan Pérez Jolote's identity as an outsider in mainstream mestizo culture is superseded by his sense of himself as an outsider in San Juan Chamula. Hence, he constantly tries to prove his loyalty to the community and its customs.

For example, he relates the difficulties he encounters in trying to convince the parents of the girl he wants to marry that he has returned to San Juan Chamula for good. He assures them that despite his knowledge of Spanish and mestizo customs, he will follow Chamula traditions and contribute to the community. Yet as Sylvia Bigas Torres notes, his readjustment to village life is never fully satisfactory, as he ceases to typify traditional village life and simply becomes "a human being lost between two irreconcilable and mutually hostile worlds" (253). Yet this anguish is something the reader must intuit, for not once does Juan Pérez Jolote express outrage at the way he has been treated or a sense that the social and economic relations between *indios* and *ladinos* could be different. In the introduction and throughout the text, the narrator remains ambivalent, even fatalistic, about the changes in Tzotzil culture brought about by increasing contact with national culture.

As the narrative draws to a close, Juan Pérez Jolote describes the corruption of ladino municipal authorities. He explains their monopoly on the liquor trade and their domination over the community's civil affairs. Juan Pérez Jolote's picture of the federal government's influence is equally bleak: he relates his brief employment as part of a rural education program, musing that after three years of teaching "a few words of Spanish and some letters so that [the Chamulans] could learn to read," the program is eliminated. Now, when people want to learn Spanish, he explains, "they buy *aceite guapo* [beautiful oil] in the drug stores in San Cristóbal, because they say taking it helps one learn to speak Spanish" (112).

It is this deadpan style of narration that leaves the question unresolved as to whether Juan Pérez Jolote is critical of the structures that control Chamulan village life or simply observes them as inevitable. Pozas later characterizes the Tzotziles of San Juan Chamula as "afraid of life" (4). In *Juan Pérez Jolote*, he creates a profile of a man and a community victimized by the caste relations between indios and ladinos. By his own account, Juan Pérez Jolote has to relearn how to be Indian, and he takes his cues as much from his own community as from the ladino authorities who fix the economic and social relations between San Juan Chamula and the rest of the world. While Pozas introduces the novel idea that "being Indian" is not a simple matter of birth, but of self-identification, the flat style in which it is narrated reinforces the stereotype of indigenous passivity and resignation to those oppressive caste relations.

In contrast with the deadpan Juan Pérez Jolote, the charismatic first-person Tzeltal narrator of *Los hombres verdaderos* (Castro, 1959) weaves a delirious and richly textured path of discovery of his place in the cosmos, in his community of Oxchuc, Chiapas, and in the national project of modernization and planned acculturation. The Earth, the universe, and the frightening and fascinating world of the ladinos delight his senses as he stretches out to feel his surroundings in passages such as the following:

> When I first learned to think, I was four years old. Just like that, as if drunk, I saw it all. The mountain ranges, the hills, they astonished me when I saw them from afar. Blue mountains, valleys, and the expanse of sky! (9)

As an optimistic young man reflecting on his childhood and young adulthood, the narrator, whose name we never learn, is sentimental and sensual. He becomes easily distracted, going off on tangents or becoming sidetracked by the immediate reality that surrounds him as he tells his story. For example, in the middle of a tale, he suddenly exclaims, "Well, as it happened . . ." or, "Careful! There's a snake over there!" The text is infused with the immediacy and spontaneity of this type of oral discourse, with its false starts and meandering plotting of events in time and space. Transitions such as "until one day," "another year went by," and "the moon made its rounds several times," further enhance the reader's illusion of partaking in the intimacy of conversation, drawn into an alluring linguistic and cognitive world.

Yet unlike Pozas's narrator, who corresponds to a flesh-and-blood individual who spoke into a tape recorder, Castro's Tzeltal narrator is a composite of many individuals who shared their stories with him while he was conducting fieldwork. Having collected material from various informants, he then organized them into what appear to be the coherently ordered experiences and observations of an individual speaker. Whereas Pozas spoke with and recorded the voice of Juan Pérez Jolote in Spanish, Castro collected his material for *Los hombres verdaderos* in Tzeltal and then translated it into Spanish.[5]

This technique of transferring the syntactical structures of his informants' speech into written Spanish conveys the intersubjectivity of Tzeltal and other Mayan languages. Carlos Lenkersdorf explains that in Tojolabal and other Mayan languages, there is not one subject and one object in a sentence, as in Spanish or English, but two subjects that interact.[6] Hence, instead of reading something like "we took the path," in this novel we find expressions such as "we and the path came to know one another" (59). Instead of "I don't know if you are telling the truth. I am going to think about it; tomorrow I'll tell you what I think," we find "I don't know if it is your truth, the one you speak, so I will think about it, to see what my heart says; tomorrow I will tell you what I am to say" (85). This is not the broken Tarzan Spanish of foundational indigenista fictions; rather, it is an attempt to render the ways in which indigenous linguistic and cognitive structures alter Spanish in its popular usage in Mexico. The profoundly different ideas about the relationships between people, and between people, animals, and all things, is compellingly rendered in passages such as the following:

> And from our conversations, as if instead of spreading words we were offering flowering water, as if distilled spirits had hidden our eyes but washed through our brains, like that, deliriously, we were getting closer to the earth, getting to know the earth, always new and with vertigo, and getting closer to the beings of the earth, people, animals, plants; moving with every other word, with each new idea as it came to us, drinking it up anew. One by one we were becoming part of the voice of our parents and grandparents, our aunts and uncles. And our language joined in with the language of the world. (20)

This effect is achieved as Castro forces the Spanish language to adopt this intersubjective syntactical structure, instead of forcing the inter-subjectivity of Tzeltal to conform to a syntax that sounds more common in standard published Spanish. This "narrative transculturation" (Rama, 1982), as a grafting of the creative and metaphorical features of Tzeltal speech onto the Spanish language, conveys an animistic vision of people and things. Hence, we find synesthetic expressions such as "The fly buzzed, as if drunk on the wind" (58), "We lit the fire to heat some tortillas. And the conversation fired up as well," and "With the sun, my shadow gave more of itself; it stretched out along the path tripping over the stones" (142).

The narrator's voice is overlaid with the voices of his parents and companions, and of parallel characters like the sun and moon. As the narrator tells the creation myths told to him by his mother and grandfather, their voices emerge in the text as well. These mythic events exist on the same temporal and spatial plane as everyday events, reflecting the narrator's unfolding knowledge of the world, which he registers with delight, as here:

And I began to discover the true nature of things. [My grandfather] told me that those who spoke best, those to whom our true language gave all its secrets, had a *ts'unún*, a hummingbird, for an animal soul.

"Is it true what you say to me, grandpa?" I asked, so that I could fly straight into the heart of his voice. (38)

Los hombres verdaderos is, like *Juan Pérez Jolote*, a coming-of-age story. We have seen that the juncture between childhood and adolescence was traumatic for Juan Pérez Jolote. He was abused by his father, enslaved, and then falsely imprisoned. In contrast, the narrator of *Los hombres verdaderos* relates the intersection of his childhood and adolescence with amusement. After having gotten a taste of schooling in his pueblo, he runs away with a friend to an Indian school in Amatenango del Valle. Although he is cruelly abused, once even forced to stay in bed for twelve days for having spoken Tzeltal with a classmate, he admires his schoolmasters and quickly gains their favor.

Even when he works as a migrant laborer (*enganchado*) on the plantations, he notices that the ladino foremen treat him better than the other workers because he speaks Spanish. Still, he is often reminded that no matter how much he identifies with the world of the ladinos, to them he is still just an Indian like any other. He awakens to this fact while working at a coffee plantation, when he is mistaken for a native of San Juan Chamula. As a seasoned migrant worker, he is accustomed to the drudgery, alienation, and humiliation of plantation work, which he recalls with painstaking detail. Thus, he is heartened and surprised when a ladino foreman calls him by his own name and entrusts the young protagonist with the job of carrying heavy mule packs. His enthusiasm for the new boss dampens, however, when he calls him the generic ladino name for the Tzotzil villagers who inhabit the valleys surrounding San Cristóbal de las Casas, regardless of whether or not they hail from San Juan Chamula. The boss addresses him thusly:

"Okay, little Chamula!"
Chamulita? That's what ladinos call the *winiketik* from Chamo, a town near Jobel [San Cristóbal]. . . . That ladino didn't know our people very well: *jo'on oxchujk'on.* . . . I am from Oxchuc!
I didn't say anything to him. I just said, "Okay boss *ajwalil!*" (81)

The narrator expresses resistance to having his identity constituted from outside, refusing to be taken for a generic Indian.

Having entered this cycle of debt peonage on the lowland coffee plantations at a young age, the narrator is not surprised to be housed in a long adobe shack with Tojolabales, Tzotziles, Mames, and other Tzeltales. Although he can sometimes get the gist of the other workers' languages, he associates with people from his own village or Tzeltal villages near his own. Still, the narrator has no difficulty identifying himself as Tzeltal even as he seeks to learn Spanish and ladino customs. Unlike the Chamula Juan Pérez Jolote, this fictional Oxchuquero finds no conflict between being Tzeltal and taking part in the life of the nation.

He passionately reflects on the lessons he has learned as well as on the injustices of the *kaxlanes* (whites) who own almost every inch of land in all directions as far as the eye can see:

> My heart learned that the little plot of land I worked was not enough. I decided to take the road down, down toward a nearby hacienda in search of work. . . . Those lands I worked down there, they yielded plenty of fruits under my farming tools, under my *luk*. But these lands were—had once been—the old communal lands of our people in Oxchuc. It was impossible to comprehend how it happened that the ladinos took this land from our great town of the three knots, only because they had embargoed it, as they say in Spanish, taking it from our people, we who could never quite understand how those tricky laws worked, the *mantalil* written on paper that could be read in many different ways, depending on what greed-filled eyes wanted to see in them. . . . We, the people of the true language, children of this earth, we who lost our papers containing our ancestors' land titles, we also had our own laws that we respected, written or not, and we never used them carelessly. . . . But now we only had nakedness and cold with which to defend ourselves! . . . in Tzeltal homes we felt only hunger then; the smallest, the most miserable strips of land, that was what was left to the true peoples from around here: the ladino wanted everything else for himself, and even these last shreds of the world if that were possible. Sometimes, as far as the eye could see along the old paths, the fields lay fallow, and the hands of the true people could not touch them. How many of us were wounded and how many pursued by dogs when we were found cultivating lands that were no longer considered ours. . . . We needed to eat, and we contracted ourselves out to work their farms, and the work kept getting harder. (93–94)

At the end of Pozas's tale, Jolote is lost to alcoholism; Pozas suggests that he has become acculturated, yes, but as a dependent and passive tool of regional power structures. His acculturation was not planned but was an accident of history, and his destiny is to become the stereotype of the Indian that Pozas had hoped to dismantle. In *Los hombres verdaderos*, in contrast, the narrator understands his personal struggles in the context of wider historical forces. What makes this ethnographic coming-of-age story fit so well within the prerogatives of state-sponsored indigenismo and what makes it a novel that celebrates the INI's regional Center in the Tzotzil-Tzeltal region is its portrayal of the federal government's role in ameliorating these injustices through planned acculturation. At the close of his tale, the narrator optimistically awaits the arrival of a new schoolteacher to his village. The narrator muses about his bright future:

> Dusk. I have arrived at the town of the three knots, Oxchuc. I have stopped to rest before I walk the last stretch to the lands that my boss now owns. I want to think about how I will talk to him [the local ladino landowner] when I see him again.
> I'll go back to my corner of land, to my hillside home. There, next to my garden, I'll keep my ears open. I think the people who said they'd come will arrive soon, and I want to receive them; I want to get to know them.
> The night is cold: the Milky Way shines brighter than ever. When the light of the sun, the light of *xutil* warms me, I will begin my journey anew. I will follow the path of my true people. (187)

In his doctoral dissertation, written under the supervision of Carlo Antonio Castro, César Rodríguez Chicharro highlights the ways in which "Castro's Tzeltal" has benefited from post-revolutionary social reforms and from federal rural education programs in particular. Chicharro states: "Castro's hero learned Spanish in his village school and the boarding school at Amatenango. He reaped the benefits of the Revolution" (118). For Chicharro, this narrator is an exemplary Indian, judged more favorably than Juan Pérez Jolote because he is as "authentic" as he is "cooperative." Unlike Juan Pérez Jolote, he has grown up primarily within his own region, "his thoroughly indigenous personality having been formed within the institutions of his own group" (118). Ironically, the perfect acculturation specimen is not an Indian per se, but is instead a character in this ethnographic novel, a character formed from a composite of several informants. Although the narrator of *Los hombres verdaderos* may appear more lifelike, more three-dimensional than Juan Pérez Jolote, he is actually more fictional, the amalgam of various informants whose words were transcribed, translated, and resequenced by Castro.

In both of these proto-testimonial texts, the indigenous narrators are given some degree of agency to express their own themes and mental processes. Even so, we cannot ascertain where the authors' perspective ends and that of the indigenous interlocutors begins. As with foundational indigenista texts, the narrator's ability to represent indigenous reality is not overtly questioned. Unlike foundational indigenista novels, however, these ethnographic coming-of-age stories feature indigenous narrators as subjects and protagonists of national history, though their protagonism is circumscribed by the adverse conditions of isolation and exploitation into which they were born.

Both of these texts feature an indigenous first-person narrator, either a real individual whose voice is taped and then transcribed, as in the case of *Juan Pérez Jolote*, or a composite of informants who are members of a particular community, as in the case of *Los hombres verdaderos*. In each case, the use of an indigenous first-person narrator lends a sense of immediacy and intimacy lacking in previous indigenista narratives. Indirectly, this narrative technique introduces the problem of authorial credibility. Here, the author appears to be a passive vehicle while the narrator gains some degree of authorial control.

Whereas in foundational indigenista texts indigenous spiritual practices are represented negatively as incoherent and fragmented superstitions, in these proto-testimonial narratives they are described by an indigenous first-person narrator, for whom they form part of a more-or-less organic and coherent cognitive framework. This narrative frame reflects the growing importance of cultural relativism in anthropological theory. However, it also effectively hides the problem of mediation, creating the illusion that the subaltern subject can "speak" through the author. Anticipating Rigoberta Menchú's testimonio published by Elizabeth Burgos Debray, the power to shape both the narrative and its reception is still out of reach for the indigenous narrator-informants of each of these texts. The role of the non-indigenous interlocutor as a mediator of indigenous voices is thus tacitly undermined, as are the traditionally held distinctions between the forms and functions attributed to literary versus social scientific texts, between truth and story.

Oficio de tinieblas *as Ethnohistorical Coming-of-age Story*

Rosario Castellanos's *Oficio de tinieblas* is unique among indigenista novels because it adheres to the formal conventions of the genre, yet ultimately critiques the state-sponsored planned acculturation program of indigenismo in which Castellanos participated. The novel is set in an indeterminate historical moment, blending events from both the Chamula revolt of 1867 and President Cárdenas's visit to Chiapas in 1936.

Its ideological ambivalence with respect to indigenista cultural politics is reflected in the troubled intercultural relationships between indigenous and ladino characters. Like mirror-image dysfunctional family dramas, the forty intercalated chapters narrating life in the Tzotzil village of San Juan Chamula and the neighboring provincial capital of San Cristóbal de las Casas involve attempts by female characters to transcend rigid family hierarchies imposed by domineering patriarchal figures.

Through relationships between white and indigenous female characters, Castellanos explores the connection between caste exploitation and the subjugation of women in patriarchy. The text examines the possibilities for transcultural relationships, for solidarity and intimacy between indigenous and white characters and especially, between indigenous and white women. As with Castellanos's earlier *Balún Canán* (1959), in *Oficio de tinieblas* an essentialized white feminine otherness is conceived as a way to gain access to the secrets of an equally essentialized indigenous otherness.

Oficio opens with a majestic retelling of the Tzotzil foundation myth of the village of San Juan Chamula, in which a pre-conquest San Juan, leader of an exodus from Palenque, transforms the grazing white sheep into stones to build his church in the palm of the valley.[7] Departing from Tzotzil versions of this myth, the narrator wryly considers that the Spanish conquest and the imposition of the Spanish language, *castilla*, by the *gente de razón* (people of reason but also, people who are *in the right*) was necessary to give meaning to this otherwise perplexing event:

> But the tribes that populated the valley of Chamula, the Tzotzil or bat people, didn't know how to interpret that sign. Neither the oldest ancients, nor the men of great wisdom could explain what was going on. All was confusing, stammering, dreamy, closing eyelids, fainting arms, and fearful gestures. That's why later, other men came. And these men came as if from another world. They wore the sun on their faces and spoke a haughty language, a language that seizes the heart of all who hear it. A language, not like Tzotzil, spoken in dreams, but a language used as an iron instrument of domination, weapon of conquest, point of the whip that is the law. But how, if not in Spanish, could orders be pronounced and sentencing declared? And how to punish and how to praise if not in Spanish? (9)

The narrator implies that before the world became "ordered" or "made rational" by the Spanish conquerors, history did not exist, because language as a tool for domination was inconceivable.[8] Power is constructed and maintained through the imposition of one language onto another, making the imposed version of reality appear to be the only possible one.

Can castilla, that language of conquest, be used as a vehicle to rewrite, to agitate and dislodge the white supremacist, patriarchal myths and histories of Highland Chiapas, the cemented justification for racist and patriarchal domination? How has it been determined that only Spanish is capable of organizing and giving meaning to indigenous myths and history? The conquerors and their progeny, who enslaved the "protean" Chamulans with their "stinging, whiplike language," have rewritten this Tzotzil myth of the foundation of San Juan Chamula to correspond to their own teleology. This Tzotzil foundational myth is infused with syncretism, as can be seen with the transformation of Quetzalcoatl into San Juan and the presence of sheep, which were brought by the Spanish colonizers. From this initial palimpsest of indigenous and Hispanic foundation myths begins a complex interrogation of the mechanisms of white, patriarchal domination and indigenous and feminine resistance.

This mythic valley of San Juan Chamula is home to Catalina Díaz Puiljá, one of the novel's four female protagonists. Led by Catalina, the women make an early morning journey to San Cristóbal to sell their wares. On the outskirts of the ladino city, they are attacked by *atajadoras*, poor mestiza women who steal their goods, throwing coins at them in order to maintain the illusion that an exchange, rather than a robbery, has taken place.[9] Young Marcela escapes the attack, but is subject to a worse affront to her dignity once she arrives in San Cristóbal. As she peddles her clay pots from door to door, she is beckoned to enter the home of Leonardo Cifuentes, the novel's principal antagonist. A stock character in any indigenista novel, Cifuentes is the prototypical *hacendado*: an arrogant, powerful landowner with an unbridled lust for domination. Marcela is cornered by Cifuentes's sinister go-between Mercedes Solórzano, an aging mestiza prostitute, and raped by Cifuentes. The reader is given to understand that the raping of young Tzotzil women is a common scenario in the Cifuentes household. From this violent and degrading encounter, the caste relationship binding the Tzotziles in San Juan Chamula to the *coletos* (inhabitants of San Cristóbal who claim descent from the original conquerors) in the colonial city of San Cristóbal is highlighted throughout the novel.

As with the foundational indigenista novels of the 1930s and 1940s, indigenous women's sexuality and reproduction are the catalysts for plot development in this novel. Yet unlike earlier indigenista novels, these events and predicaments (violence against women from outside as well as from inside the community) are not merely symbolic of the victimization of a collectivity. Since the omniscient narrator dwells on indigenous and ladino women characters' thoughts and actions as they cope with sexual violence and marginalization, they are more complexly developed than the male characters. The exploration of the psychological effects of male domination on the women characters and the latter's strategies of resistance are central themes in the novel.

When Marcela returns empty-handed and speechless after having been raped by Cifuentes, Catalina alone understands what has occurred. As a powerful *ilol*, or priestess, and wife of a village dignitary, she commands respect from her peers. At the same time, her childlessness marks her as an object of ridicule and suspicion and taints her status. She devises a plan to save the girl from the social disgrace of having been raped by a coleto to resolve her own problem of infertility and the social shame that accompanies it, and to find a caretaker for her younger brother. No one dares object when Catalina takes Marcela into her home and raises her mestizo son, Domingo, as her own. But as Domingo grows and strays from the domestic fire, moving into the masculine realm of life by her husband Pedro Winiktón's side in San Juan Chamula, Catalina is again left lonely and desperate for validation.

The forty intercalated chapters that make up *Oficio de tinieblas* alternately portray life from the perspective of the Cifuentes family in San Cristóbal and that of Catalina and Pedro in the neighboring Tzotzil village of San Juan Chamula. Both households are marked by scandal: in San Cristóbal, rumors abound that Leonardo killed his stepbrother in order to marry the wealthy Isabel. This story is told from the perspective of Isabel's daughter, Idolina, an adolescent girl who feigns paralysis and dreams up schemes of revenge on her mother and dreaded stepfather from her sickbed. Meanwhile, in San Juan Chamula, Marcela gives birth to Domingo during an eclipse. A struggle over the interpretation of this prodigious event and, ultimately, over the power to lead the community, ensues between Catalina and the village's traditionally male-dominated civil-religious order, which operates loosely according to the dictates of the bishop of San Cristóbal.

The relationship between these two communities is profoundly affected by the arrival of a cosmopolitan couple from Mexico City. Fernando Ulloa is an impassioned and idealistic agronomist sent by the Cárdenas government to implement land reform. His common-law wife Julia, a lusty and uninhibited social climber, has an affair with Cifuentes in a failed attempt to ingratiate herself to the local high society. Each in his or her own way, these characters challenge the rigid social hierarchies that keep white women and indigenous people silent, invisible, and disposable while allowing characters such as Cifuentes to act with cruelty and impunity. The coletos' provincialism is highlighted by their unfavorable reactions to these outsiders. Local elites see Fernando and Julia as threatening to rigid social mores and long-standing caste relationships, which affirm the superiority of whites over Indians and men over women.

Two events serve to place the novel within the context of the Lázaro Cárdenas presidency of the 1930s: First, Pedro, has his hopes for justice ignited while he is at work in a lowland coffee plantation. President Cárdenas gives a speech in which he promises land reform and protection for indigenous peasants from the landowners' abusive treatment. Shortly thereafter, the agronomist Fernando Ulloa is sent to highland Chiapas as a representative of the Cárdenas administration in order to oversee the implementation of federal land and labor reforms. Through the character of Fernando, Castellanos explores the role of the urban intellectual as a well-intentioned yet ineffectual mediator between the state and indigenous groups and, by extension, between Mexico City and the provinces. The disjuncture between Fernando's good intentions and the coletos' efforts to impede him in his task allow Castellanos to subtly critique the indigenista project in which she had participated. When Pedro returns to San Juan Chamula, he befriends Fernando, seeing in him an ally in his struggle against the coleto landowners. Yet while Fernando's concept of justice is tied to the constitution and the rule of law as articulated by the federal government, Pedro yearns for a deeper vengeance against his oppressors. The misunderstanding that later arises between these two men hinges on their different understandings of the meaning of justice.

Fernando is characterized as hopelessly naïve; when he allies himself with the Tzotziles, he is immediately cast as an outlaw by the local caciques, because their laws have no correlation with those of the federal government but are instead upheld by their mercenary "white guards" or private henchmen. Ultimately, these two characters' inability to communicate their intentions leads to mutual betrayal. Frustrated by the landowners' arrogant refusal to cooperate in the land and labor reform measures, Fernando is swept up in a tide of indigenous rebellion, which is brutally avenged by the landowners. In the end, he is pegged by the local caciques as the leader of the rebellion and alienated by the Tzotziles because he has stirred their hopes for justice but could not deliver the land he had promised them.

As Pedro Winiktón gains prestige as a political leader and is heartened by Fernando's insistence that justice is finally on the side of indigenous peasants, Catalina seeks her own recognition by resuscitating an ancient cult to three stone statues. The stone gods speak through her in a cave in the small hamlet of Tzajal Hemel outside San Juan Chamula. When the villagers abandon the Catholic church in the plaza of San Juan Chamula and make frequent pilgrimages to the stone idols in the cave, the ladino priest destroys the statues. Catalina's status wanes, but she is able to recapture the people's loyalty when she gives birth to three clay figures, who continue to speak through her, this time ordering the people to cast off the yoke of ladino domination. At this point, Pedro's and Catalina's independent struggles become one.

While the action surrounding Catalina and her family unfolds in the religious and political center of San Juan Chamula and the nearby *paraje* (hamlet) of Tzajal Hemel, another plot, centered upon the sick-bed of Cifuentes's tormented stepdaughter, Idolina, and her Tzotzil wetnurse, Teresa, develops in San Cristóbal. While Fernando Ulloa's character is a vehicle for exploring the limits of the reformist project of official indigenismo, Teresa and Idolina are the characters through whom Castellanos expresses her preoccupations about writing and the silencing of women in patriarchy. What unites these two characters is their pain at the hands of Idolina's mother and stepfather, and the social isolation they both face. Idolina is literally paralyzed by anger at her mother and stepfather, who have killed her beloved father.

Through Idolina's interior monologue and conversations with Teresa, the reader gains insight into the pain of both characters: They are united by their rage against Idolina's mother and stepfather and by a bittersweet dependence; when Idolina's mother, Isabel, had been unable to breastfeed the newborn Idolina, Cifuentes kidnapped Teresa from her village to serve as Idolina's wet nurse. Unable to produce enough milk for Idolina and her own baby, she was forced to let him die so that Idolina might live. Teresa's breast milk both unites them and symbolizes the violent caste relations that keep their fates tied to each other in a perverse adult-servant–child-master relationship.

Idolina is capricious and insensitive to Teresa's pain, but she has come to interpret the events of the household and of what little she sees of the world around her in the Tzotzil language and through the lens of Tzotzil myths, legends, and prophesies. Idolina's mother shamefully admits that Idolina "learned the [Tzotzil] language before Spanish" (141). With Idolina as her interlocutor, Teresa keeps the Tzotzil oral tradition alive. Despite, or perhaps because of her confinement in the Cifuentes home, Teresa identifies with her capricious charge. Although Idolina is often fickle and cruel in her dependence on Teresa, each is the only living being with whom the other has any physical and spiritual connection.

As I suggested above, Idolina's impotent rage, which she unleashes on all who surround her, especially her mother, stems from the tragic loss of her father at the hands of her malevolent stepfather, Leonardo Cifuentes. Idolina feigns a paralyzing illness in a passive-aggressive attempt to exact revenge on her mother, who acted as the accomplice to the murder. As outsiders who are powerless to leave this cycle of humiliating enclosure, Idolina and Teresa cling to each other, plotting to exact revenge on their common enemies. The precarious solidarity between them dissolves, however, as Idolina reaches puberty and struggles to find her place in coleto society. She cruelly rejects Teresa's nurturance, clinging instead to the enchanting Julia Acevedo, Fernando's common-law wife. Idolina soon realizes that Julia's affections toward her have been part of a scheme to get closer to Leonardo. Once Julia has become his mistress, Idolina is forgotten, driving the girl to a state of loneliness and paranoia that bring her to write a letter of protest.

> The guilty ones are out of reach. How can she punish them? She invents spells, recites them. If only her nana, Teresa, were here! But she quiets down when she realizes her words have no meaning, no use. And she returns to where she started: the crime, a crime of such magnitude that her head explodes. She stands up. It's midnight and the embers in the fireplace have burned out. Stumbling, she moves toward the light and turns it on. But the project that motivated her to get out of bed has vanished before the candle's weak and trembling flame. What did she want? Oh, yes, to complain, to protest. But not tomorrow; centuries could go by before dawn. She anxiously searches for a piece of paper and pencil. She who can barely write is filling page after page with the giant, undisciplined handwriting of one accustomed to occupying her hands with other tasks. It's a tumultuous outpouring of words, a childish confession, the last scream of someone drowning. When she finishes she is trembling as if from physical exertion. She folds the letter and stuffs it in an envelope. Only then does she realize she has no one to address it to. Before snuffing out the candle she lights one of the corners of the manuscript. Aided by this sudden flash of light, she returns to bed.
>
> Now she shivers in the cold and the momentary relief the writing gave her has disappeared. (201–202)

Here, writing is described as a physical and mental convulsion, as a way to direct rage outward instead of against the self. That the fire has gone out in the stove symbolizes Idolina's alienation from humanity. Having driven Teresa away with her abuse, Idolina has no one to keep the fire lit and no interlocutor. Therefore, her writing is conceived as a supplement to human communication, a possible way to overcome her alienation and sense of powerlessness. She tries in vain to invent an interlocutor, but burns her manuscript when she realizes she has no one to whom she might address the letter, using its ephemeral light to return to her bed. She is desperate to take part in the social world, but she wants to do it on her own terms. As she becomes aware of her lack of social autonomy, she retreats back into her sick bed and back into the world of Teresa's Tzotzil prophesies and legends.

Although here Idolina burns the letter, having no one to send it to, at the close of the novel it mysteriously ends up on Fernando's night table, where Julia finds and reads it. It must be Idolina's letter, which gives sordid details of Julia's affair with Leonardo, because the handwriting is described in similar terms, as infantile and uncertain: "A cheap envelope, poor penmanship, ignorant spelling. . . . That vulgar handwriting looked as if it had been scrawled by someone completing a primary school lesson" (290).

The novel depicts these two worlds as violently interconnected. The coleto world dominates the Tzotzil world through writing; in turn, the Tzotziles fight back by developing their own language of resistance. Aside from alphabetic texts such as Idolina's letter, land titles, and military plans, the intercalated stories are woven together by objects that function as pictographic "texts"—as prophesies and means of reclaiming history, memory, and the future for those who are rendered powerless by the imposition of a patriarchal and racist language and epistemology. Doris Sommer might consider these as alternative means of communication, as "irruptions of messianic presence that pierce through 'empty and homogenous' secular time" (5).[10] Teresa reads the ashes in Idolina's fireplace for a connection to her Tzotzil communal past and clues about the future; a richly woven Guatemalan scarf that Leonardo gives to Julia makes its way to Catalina's altar, wrapped around her idols and acquiring powerful associations as it travels back and forth between Mayan and ladino worlds, symbolizing both a pan-Mayan unity as well as the interconnectedness of all women who struggle for independence from male domination; Idolina's letters denounce her stepfather's murderous crime and foretell the Chamulan uprising.[11]

In *Prospero's Daughter* (1995), Joanna O'Connell notes that "Castellanos' writing examines the responses of individuals as they try to negotiate between competing and contradictory constructions of identity, . . . map[ping] the complex intersections of two kinds of inequality: the situation of women in sexist societies and that of indigenous peoples in the Americas, through the example of the Maya in Mexico, whose oppression is rooted in colonialism and the persistence of colonial relations" (23). O'Connell likens Castellanos's moral challenge to that of Prospero's daughter Miranda in Shakespeare's *The Tempest*; like Miranda, Castellanos finds herself in the "'(ambiguously) non-hegemonic' situation of women writers who are interpolated through their class and racial position as owing allegiance to the colonizer, but who, as women, are also positioned in crucial ways as subordinate" (viii). O'Connell argues that Castellanos created "hybrid texts, palimpsests of domination and resistance, [which] are also sites of discursive struggle over meaning between Maya and ladino constitutions of community through memory" (93).

Published in 1962, just before criticism of indigenismo as a state policy of cultural and economic appropriation begins to stir, the themes and characters of this novel reflect a growing sense that if the indigenista project is to represent the interests of indigenous communities instead of those of national elites, its proponents must wrest it from the cooptation by capitalist and state interests and contemplate alternatives to its patronizing stance toward the indigenous peoples of Mexico. While *Oficio de tinieblas* constitutes a strong condemnation of the oppression of the Tzotzil people of San Juan Chamula by the coleto society of San Cristóbal, it is also an exploration of the ideological contradictions of an indigenismo that straddles socialist and capitalist notions of modernity and progress. Castellanos's questioning of the role of indigenista intellectuals precipitates the collapse of the genre. The novel challenges indigenista writers and bureaucrats to examine their own position as brokers between national elites and local indigenous groups.

In this novel, the connection between white women and indigenous communities ultimately proves fragile. Catalina's religious movement has been driven underground and the novel closes with Teresa back in her place, at Idolina's bedside (368). While Castellanos (as well as Marie-Odile Marion, as we shall see in the following chapter) carves out a literary space for herself within a patriarchal system by emphasizing a biological connection between women across class and ethnic antagonisms, the women characters that populate her text are, paradoxically, notable for their rejection of or inability to fulfill traditional feminine roles, perhaps mirroring these writers' difficulties in gaining a voice in the male-dominated field of intellectual production.

Indigenismo and Narrative Transculturation

Alberto Moreiras distinguishes between two uses of the term "transculturation": the first, anthropological and the second, literary. In the first sense, Moreiras argues, it describes a "cultural mixing (some acquisition, some loss, and some creation are always ingredients in it). And then, 'transculturation' also refers to a different use as a critical concept: that is, to an active, self-conscious use of it as a tool for aesthetic or critical production (or the analysis thereof)."[12] For Moreiras, the task of the theorist who contemplates literary production must not simply be to identify and celebrate instances of narrative transculturation, since "transculturation is in itself always already transculturated, . . . as historically produced as the phenomena it would seek to interpret."[13]

According to Moreiras, in *El zorro de arriba y el zorro de abajo* (1971) José María Arguedas does not pretend to marry heterogeneous linguistic-symbolic universes, but instead, contemplates, horrified, the abyss between them. Moreiras warns against the dangers of trying to find in narrative transculturation an escape from or transcendence of social antagonisms:

> Transculturation—that is, the macroprocess by means of which elements of one culture are naturalized in another culture, not without undergoing some changes during the process—of course insists on conciliation, conjunction, and dialectical unification of the global cultural field. It is a productive model, but it is also a model which must work and even feed upon the systematic erasure of that which does not fit into it. And this Rama knew well. . . . Transculturation is a part of the ideology of cultural productionism, indeed a systemic part of a Western metaphysics of production, which still retains a strong colonizing grip on the cultural field.[14]

In a similarly cautionary tone, John Beverley describes transculturation as a theology, considered by Angel Rama (and Ortíz before him) to be "necessary in the last instance for national popular culture in Latin America." In *Subalternity and Representation*, he contends that:

> Rama cannot conceptualize ideologically or theoretically movements for indigenous identity, rights, and/or territorial autonomy that develop their own organic intellectuals and (literary or non-literary) cultural forms—forms that not only do not depend necessarily on a narrative transculturation but in many cases feel obliged to resist or contradict such a narrative (by the same token, he was unable to conceptualize the emergence of a grassroots women's movement in Latin America). The idea of transculturation expressed in both Ortiz and Rama is a fantasy of class, gender, and racial reconciliation (in, respectively, liberal and social-democratic forms).[15]

Although some critics have considered narrative transculturation to comprise a more "democratizing" or anti-elitist literary practice, the field of literary production in which it is elaborated (much like official indigenista discourse) is still one of "conflictive heterogeneity" or a closed circuit from which marginalized elements and agents—in this case, indigenous peoples themselves, as an ontological category—are filtered out. Since this production unfolds without the participation of the subaltern referent, the conditions for the development of a dynamic relationship between dominant and subaltern cultural formations, a relationship that would actually work to disintegrate the structures that delineate the dominant/subaltern binary, run up against serious limitations. What is "lost in the translation" is the possibility that those with a Western or Europeanized worldview might not be able to hold on to the position of ultimate articulator of social identities, might not have the last word or the perfect vantage point from which to look at the vast world of cultural differences.

O'Connell explains that while Rama and Antonio Cornejo Polar are concerned with the role of literature in the reproduction of social power in Latin America, "Rama posits the relationship between cultural modes as fusion while Cornejo Polar sees it as one of conflict."[16] Can narrative transculturation offer a "counterrationality" to the hegemonic discourse of ethnicity and ethnic-social conflict, as some critics have suggested? Or is it, as Moreiras has argued, a "war machine, feeding on cultural difference, whose principal function is the reduction of radical cultural heterogeneity,"[17] a project that, when apparently most successful at undercutting Western rationality and bourgeois hegemony, is also most doomed to reinforce it. Like Martín Lienhard, O'Connell expresses an optimism that is more restrained than that of Rama, but less skeptical than Moreiras and Beverley. Both Lienhard and O'Connell hold out hope for the possibility that "alternative cultural practices, or subjugated knowledges, might potentially produce political subjects within the nationalist context, subjects whose history of resistance might enable counterhegemonic projects."[18]

In the case of Mexican indigenismo, there is an additional problem, an ideological by-product of this initial contradiction produced by the reduction of the indigenous referent to a sign, a one-dimensional, generic figure: indigenista writers, artists, and administrators are enmeshed in the post-revolutionary state apparatus. Their ideological function, whether recognized or not, is to absorb and redirect peasant and working-class aspirations for social justice into the aspirations of the single party state, which claims for itself the ability to administer modernity and revolutionary justice. According to Rama, the most troubling aspect of indigenista cultural production is that while it masquerades as a radical project of vindication of indigenous collective rights, it is actually a refined instrument of bourgeois hegemony.

Thus, indigenista writers tend to construct a Manichean universe of economic and moral exploitation. The newly urbanized middle and upper classes—which create and consume indigenista fiction—are consistently placed on a moral high ground, exonerated so that they can be the privileged disseminator and audience of this literature. As in official indigenista discourse, multiple layers of exploitation born of national and transnational capitalism are drastically oversimplified in order to stage an epic moral struggle between white landowners and Indians. The literary and political discourses elaborated around indigenous peoples' existence address cosmopolitan middle-class readers, certainly not the villainous white landholders or the exploited illiterate indigenous peasants these novels invariably portray. The indigenista literary project, then, is at an impasse: On one hand, it cannot radically alter dominant stereotypes of the indigenous *other*, because the absence of the referent leads to the projection of Europeanized cognitive and aesthetic imperatives onto its fictionalized indigenous landscapes. On the other hand, indigenismo also fails to represent how, in post-revolutionary Mexico, indigenous peoples have often been used as pawns in the struggle between the semi-feudal oligarchy and the emerging national bourgeoisie, whose hegemony depends on the construction of a homogeneous national identity and the subordination of indigenous identities.

The critical dilemma of the indigenista intellectual, as suggested by Castellanos in *Oficio de tinieblas*, is how to bring about political change (namely, land reform) in an increasingly anti-revolutionary atmosphere, along with the paradox of having to understand oneself as a possible impediment to such reform; given the bourgeois turn of events of the Mexican Revolution, the non-indigenous, urban intellectual awkwardly finds him- or herself dependent on political elites who justify their newfound power by claiming to embody revolutionary ideals even as they seek national homogenization and capitalist modernization above justice and equality.

Conclusion

The foundational indigenista novels discussed in the previous chapter featured omniscient, third-person narrators who positioned themselves as exterior and superior to the indigenous communities they portrayed. In them, we find three notable features: first, frequent authorial interventions that serve to "explain" the behaviors, practices, and mentalities of the indigenous characters; second, little or no engagement with the indigenous or oral-popular linguistic and cognitive structures characteristic of what Angel Rama considered "narrative transculturation"; finally, these novels feature a Manichean vision of the indigenous as morally superior yet defenseless victims of white rapacity. Doris Sommer might say that in these texts, the distance between writing subject and written object or referent "plays treacherously in a subject-centered key that overwhelms unfamiliar voices only to repeat the solitary sounds of the self."[19] Another level of analysis reveals that this apparent narrative self-confidence (what Sommer refers to as a "dangerously smug self-authorization")[20] is punctuated by moments of doubt, an ambivalence toward not only those indigenous groups but also toward the official indigenista project embraced by the institutionalized post-revolutionary state.

The waning of the foundational moment in indigenista literature and social policy, and the beginnings of a new chapter in the history of the discourse of race in post-revolutionary Mexico can be glimpsed in the texts discussed here. We have seen that these narrators cease to appear as an omniscient presence hovering above the plot, and instead become self-conscious observers, reflecting on the ways in which their authorial gaze transforms and distorts that which is represented. In ethnographic writing, there is a turn toward recording the words of indigenous informants as a means for drawing conclusions about indigenous life and consciousness. Here agency is transferred, if only partially and conditionally, to indigenous referents or interlocutors.

Although there is a change in the dynamic between the writer and the indigenous referent in both the ethnographic and ethno-historical narratives discussed here, this later indigenista cultural production is still essentially a closed circuit, wherein the writer has ultimate control over the shape of the narrative. A precise moment at which this changes is difficult to determine, since the fundamental drive present in the foundational vein—that of social reconciliation through the fantasy of alliance between indigenous peasants and the urban bourgeoisie—persists through all later forms of indigenismo and even spills over into testimonio, as we shall see in the following chapter. At the same time, these proto-testimonios show us that indigenous communities are not passive victims, but rather, actively struggle to break free from the paternalistic state and its limited imaginings about indigenous life and thought.

The narratives discussed here focus on the possibilities and problems associated with indigenous assimilation to mainstream national culture. They do not posit an alternative to it, as later indigenous testimonios do. Yet insofar as they introduce the notion of the indigenous person as an individual subject, an agent, and participant in national history, they gesture toward that later political and literary project.

Testimonio and Indigenous Struggles for Autonomy

Testimonio is a narrative form created through collaboration between a speaker who chronicles his or her experience as a member of a subaltern group and a publishing author who transcribes and shapes the speaker's oral account. As a text forged between author and speaker in a moment of grave social repression and/or collective mobilization, testimonio has carried the "small voice of history" (Guha, 1988) to within earshot of a wider reading public and has often helped to galvanize solidarity for the communities in whose name the speaker tells his or her personal account. Testimonios allow the truths of marginalized people to reach beyond a small circle of acquaintances, challenging hegemonic ideas of who can speak and in what form that communication should be conveyed.

In this chapter I consider the ways in which three testimonios narrate indigenous struggles for cultural survival and construct intercultural alternatives to indigenista literary and ethnographic conventions. In these testimonios, the connections between memory, speaking, and writing, as well as between the indigenous speaker's and the non-indigenous writer's subject positions, are blurred in the process of constructing intimate plot-driven narratives that draw readers in as if they were savoring works of fiction.

Since the 1960s, testimonio has emerged as a vital medium of social critique and literary innovation throughout Latin America, first as a chronicle of resistance to the counter-insurgency repression of the Cold War and more recently, as a call to action against neoliberal globalization. Testimonios have catalyzed popular struggles against land theft, labor exploitation, and state violence by creating national and international networks of solidarity and activism among readers. Now classic testimonios such as *Let Me Speak! Testimonio of Domitila, A Woman of the Bolivian Mines* (1970) transcribed and edited by Moema Viezzer and *I, Rigoberta Menchú, An Indian Woman in Guatemala* (1983) transcribed and edited by Elizabeth Burgos-Debray tell the story of liberation movements from the perspectives of their protagonist-narrators, showing how their personal struggles intersect with those of their communities.

In Mexico, as elsewhere in Latin America, the emergence of testimonio has raised questions about the mediatory role of intellectuals in a society characterized by deep gender, sexual, class, ethnic, linguistic, and educational stratification. Elena Poniatowska's widely read *Hasta No Verte Jesús Mío* (1969) and *La Noche de Tlatelolco* (1970) reflect the genre's prominence in contemporary Mexican letters, channeling public outrage over the post-revolutionary state's failure to bring social justice to the urban poor and its brutal repression against those who have dared to voice this outrage. Expanding on the ethnographic fieldwork methodologies of participant observation and the use of portable tape recorders by authors such as Oscar Lewis in *The Children of Sánchez* and Ricardo Pozas in *Juan Pérez Jolote* (see chap. 3), testimonio writers give primacy to their interlocutors' perspectives and modes of expression, yet shape and transform these oral accounts as they prepare them for publication in ways of which we as readers often remain unaware.

While Poniatowska's urban testimonios occupy a prominent place within the Mexican field of literary and intellectual production, testimonios that chronicle indigenous people's struggles for self-determination and cultural survival in rural Mexico have received less attention. Like the indigenista texts we have examined in previous chapters, indigenous testimonios feature non-indigenous writers as conveyors of indigenous life and consciousness; yet they depart significantly from indigenista literary and ethnographic texts, as they explicitly reject the image of indigenous communities as closed corporate entities existing outside modernity. As they blur the boundaries between ethnographer and informant as well as between author and speaker, indigenous testimonios favor the perspectives of their indigenous interlocutors. Testimonio's deconstruction of traditional monologic literary and ethnographic conventions mirrors the unraveling of indigenismo as a hegemonic discourse of race in Mexico.

Memorial del tiempo o vía de las conversaciones (1987), by Jesús Morales Bermúdez, *Entre anhelos y recuerdos* (1997), by Marie-Odile Marion, and the letters and communiqués of subcomandante Insurgente Marcos (the spokesman for the Zapatista Army of National Liberation or EZLN from 1994 to 2003) exemplify this transformation in how indigeneity is defined and imagined within the Mexican cultural imagination. What is at stake in these indigenous testimonios is not whether the indigenous people whose stories they convey will adapt to and be absorbed by national culture, as was the case with indigenista texts; rather, it is whether the non-indigenous writer-transcribers of these testimonios will cross a different kind of threshold, becoming acculturated and accepted as allies to the indigenous speakers whose oral accounts they shape into written narratives.

Produced through collaboration between non-indigenous writers and indigenous speakers, indigenous testimonios move away from the preoccupation with making indigenous people seem exotic and uncivilized to non-indigenous readers. Yet they do not simply mark an evolution from indigenismo to autonomous forms of indigenous literary expression, as they continue to be characterized by non-indigenous mediation of indigenous voices for a predominantly non-indigenous readership.[1]

These testimonio writers position themselves as listeners, acknowledging their imperfect renditions as they channel the voices of their indigenous interlocutors to their non-indigenous readers. As they address patriarchal and racist oppression as well as an imbalance of power between themselves and their indigenous interlocutors, they call attention to the limits of their interpretations of indigenous life and consciousness, revealing a deep-seated ambivalence about the methods and goals of conventional ethnographic research and literary representation.

In the course of "living with the people and their problems" (Morales Bermúdez, 1999, 13), each writer contemplates the gap between his or her own privileged social position and that of the interlocutor and struggles with the ethical choice of staying an outsider or taking part in the community's struggles for land, autonomy, and human rights. In contrast with the indigenista formula of modernization through induced assimilation, testimonial writers convey and find themselves enmeshed in indigenous peoples' struggles for cultural survival in the face of local coercion, national cooptation, and transnational plunder. Indigenous interlocutors tell of cattle ranchers, loggers, and plantation owners encroaching on their communal lands and preventing them from cultivating their milpas; they denounce the increasing military and paramilitary violence waged against their communities when they attempt to resist these predations; they tell of abusive entrepreneurs who usurp the land and treat it as a source of profit rather than a source of sustenance; finally, they tell of despotic and corrupt state and municipal authorities supported by the federal government to uphold that status quo.

To a far greater extent than with the indigenista writers discussed in previous chapters, these authors redirect the authority from which to speak about indigenous identity away from themselves and toward their indigenous interlocutors, rejecting the indigenista paradigm of social scientific expertise and benevolent acculturation. Clearly, each of the indigenista texts we have examined thus far denounces the racist legacies of colonialism in contemporary society; yet while indigenista writers cast the postrevolutionary state as redeemer and benefactor of indigenous people, even when that state is seen as imperfect, indigenous testimonios point directly to the government as the architect of indigenous disenfranchisement.

Critique of Indigenismo

The rejection of official indigenismo from the fringes of the social scientific establishment surfaced in 1970 with the publication of *De eso que llaman antropología mexicana* edited by Arturo Warman. The authors of this anthology, as well as many other social scientists, represented a new generation of anthropologists critical of the National Indigenist Institute (INI), charging that the agency's primary function had become that of ensuring political and economic control of indigenous communities. These social scientists accused indigenistas of bureaucratizing applied anthropology and of inhibiting and co-opting indigenous peoples' engagement in national society. They argued that INI rural development initiatives displaced indigenous communities and subordinated them to the state rather than liberating them from colonial servitude. They also denounced the increasing military and paramilitary repression of communities that attempted to protest or resist these incursions.[2]

These academic critiques coalesced with and were inspired by new peasant organizations that drew on their collective indigenous identity as a strategy of mobilization. In the face of mounting commercial and military pressures, particularly in the southern and southeastern states where indigenous populations are largest and poverty is most appalling, grassroots leaders worked to recast the terms of debate regarding indigenous peoples' inclusion in national affairs. Staking their claims for land and autonomy on their historically constituted collective rights as indigenous pueblos, they gained adherents among many of the non-indigenous intellectuals critical of state-sponsored indigenismo. Indigenous testimonio thus emerged as a medium through which indigenous organizers began to collaborate with non-indigenous social scientists and activists in order to foster spaces of collective association and critique outside the tutelage of the ruling party structure.

At the same time, the federal government strove to showcase Mexico's modernity by hosting the summer Olympics in 1968, the World Cup in 1970, and the Pan-American Games in 1972. In the literary field, the Latin American "boom" cast a golden light on Mexico's most prolific writers, Octavio Paz and Carlos Fuentes. Novels, films, and television shows moved away from nostalgic representations of a pre-revolutionary social order and focused instead on themes of urban life and social mobility. In popular films such as *Los caifanes* (1966) and *Mecánica nacional* (1971), Mexico City became the main character; the countryside was seen as a foreign country—a quaint, stagnant backwater.

Yet for all the glamour surrounding the so-called economic miracle and the boom in state-subsidized urban cultural production, it was difficult to conceal the fact that much of Mexico's celebrated modernization and industrialization had been erected on very shaky foundations. Contradictions in the political system abounded. Worker and student strikes were brutally repressed. The massacre of Tlatelolco, in which at least four hundred student protesters and bystanders were gunned down by the National Army in Mexico City in October 1968, is often considered the turning point after which the Institutional Revolutionary Party's representation of itself as the dispenser of revolutionary justice became increasingly difficult to sustain.

Mexican intellectuals divided into two camps: apologists for the Institutional Revolutionary Party (PRI) on one hand and critics on the other. Within the latter camp, testimonio played a crucial role in denouncing the government's human rights abuses and exposing the official silencing of dissenting voices. Poniatowska's *La noche de Tlatelolco* (1971) made testimonio a key vehicle of protest, providing a critical voice in a time of increasing censorship of media outlets.

As President Luis Echeverría Alvarez took office in 1970, amid hushed allegations that he had ordered the massacre, an important feature of the PRI's political strategy became that of increasing state control of the media. The government rewarded television, radio, and film executives for presenting a positive image of a democratic and prosperous Mexican society to the nation and abroad.[3] State control of media also reached into print journalism: in the mid-1970s, the government took control of the daily newspaper *Excelsior* and the weekly news magazines *El Nacional* and *Uno Más Uno* in order to keep close tabs on political debate.

Although in the 1960s and 1970s rural life may have ceased to generate the enthusiasm in the urban literary circuits it once had, social conditions in the countryside were far from static. The population soared and land was overworked and poorly distributed. For the first time since the

Cristero War in the 1920s, the Mexican armed forces were active in the surveillance and repression of popular guerilla movements. As Carlos Montemayor narrates in *Guerra en el paraíso* (1991), the government's dirty war against peasant movements led by Genaro Vázquez and Lucio Cabañas made the relationship between city and countryside extremely tense. In these circumstances, for an urban intellectual to go to the countryside to do an ethnographic study or social service was tantamount to declaring oneself a communist. There was no safe way for urban intellectuals to forge relationships with peasant leaders except within the highly controlled organizations of the state, namely the National Peasant Confederation (CNC) or the Instituto Nacional Indigenista (INI); in both cases the idea was to arrive with a mission that had been formulated from the urban center to be applied to a specific community, to infiltrate that community, identify potential subversives, and co-opt the civil-religious leadership. In terms of literary production, there would be no way to depict indigenous peasants' reality without representing the state as the antagonist, for the state had finally come to replace or at least to stand arm-in-arm with the villainous landowner. What had been the bedrock of indigenista narratives, the representation of the post-revolutionary government as benefactor and redeemer of indigenous peasants, was now losing credibility.

Globalization and the Challenges of Pluriculturalism

As the 1970s oil boom gave way to the debt crisis of the 1980s, the ruling party resorted to drastic measures to assure its hegemony and maintain the façade of democratic governance.[4] Mexico hosted the World Cup in 1986, but by this time institutionalized revolutionary nationalism had fallen into grave crisis. As President Miguel de la Madrid addressed the crowd of soccer fans, his amplified voice was drowned out by the whistles and jeers of a stadium packed with angry hecklers. This bold public embarrassment to the president, unheard of in previous years, reflected middle and working class Mexicans' desperation as a wave of devaluations had deflated wages by forty percent from their 1982 level.[5] The rage expressed in the Estadio Azteca that day made clear that the PRI's political machine and the presidency were no longer unassailable. The economic crisis was aggravated by the government's failure to respond to the humanitarian tragedy following the 1985 earthquake. The ruling party gradually ceased to anchor its control of the state in the Revolution of 1910. The nationalist narrative of a common past forged in conquest, independence, and revolution leading to a modern, prosperous future was coming undone.

In his prologue to *Memorial del tiempo o vía de las conversaciones* (1987), Jesús Morales Bermúdez explains that his decision to take up residence among the Ch'ol community in northern Chiapas in 1973 was born of the disenchantment he suffered as a result of the military coup and assassination of Salvador Allende in Chile and other challenges to the left in Mexico. It was, he explains, "an attempt to bring some coherence to the crisis that followed the student movement of 1968 and the [massacre] of Corpus Christi Thursday in 1971" (9).

Morales Bermúdez describes how this political disenchantment and the desire for a new society landed him in the jungle, where he witnessed the resurgence of pan-Mayan resistance to ethnocide that began with the 1974 Interamerican Indigenous Conference in San Cristóbal de las Casas.

He describes the process through which he came to know his Ch'ol hosts:

> For the first time, we had access to the world of the concrete; for once, as mestizos and indigenous people we became as brothers and we shared our knowledge without ulterior motives. We walked together and got soaked in the rain and we slept on the same hard floors, we shared food, pozol, sweat, and firewater. We cried for our dead. For little Dieguito that died from eating so much soil, from so much desire to return to the soil. We recited the same prayers and, even within our disbelief, we were priests when called upon to be priests. We longed for a world of justice. We learned that the local powermongers turn the soil into a conquest and that their hearts feed on our blood. (10)

In this unconventional testimonio, reconstructed from memory, the author seeks to make his written Spanish conform to a Ch'ol way of speaking *castilla* (Castillian Spanish), to represent "an indigenous modality of speaking Spanish" (10). Although much of this literary transculturation is lost in my translation to English, we can appreciate the insight this text provides into a Ch'ol perspective on the contemporary indigenous movement in Mexico. Reflecting on the reasons for his community's involvement in the 1974 Conference, the narrator explains:

> It's that there's no land for us to live on! . . . And this is because there are many whites [*caxlanes*] . . . that have pushed us off our *ejido* and have settled their horse ranches right on our ejido. . . . And in vain we go to Mexico, or we go to Tuxtla [the capital of the state of Chiapas], or we appeal to Agrarian Reform, or to the INI, or Indigenous Affairs. We try them all and find no way to fix anything. A year goes by, thirty-six years and nothing is done to fix it. An engineer

comes, a lawyer, the lawyer demands money, an agrarian delegate arrives, the agrarian delegate demands money; everyone comes to take money. . . . That's how we begin to get fed up. . . . You might not believe this, old man, but that's how once and for all we become wise, and we start getting together to prepare the celebration of Las Casas [San Cristóbal de las Casas, Chiapas]. . . . and the word went flowing through the mountains, and it now seems this time as if the word flowing through us is a fire, as if it is water flowing through the rivers, or as if it is wind flowing through every thing and goes through mountain, valley, forest, mountain range, through all the ears of those that are like us, peasant, Indian, all. (140–41)

Dispensing with the paternalistic tone of previous indigenista writers, Morales Bermúdez reveals his doubt and discomfort with the literary text he creates out of the memories of listening to Ch'ol storytellers over the course of several years. Morales Bermúdez tries to capture the feeling and structure of Ch'ol Mayan oral discourse, rendering it in a fictional Spanish that echoes the rhythm, syntax, and vocabulary of Mayan-inflected popular Spanish. Thus, he muses: "It is with great pain that I recognize that this transcription of their tales is like 'stealing' a bit of life from these peoples; perhaps it impoverishes them in some way" (13). At the same time, by the author's own admission, this text is not a transcription, but a rendition of the stories he collected, filtered through his own memory, a testimony to the virtue of listening to the voices that speak their truths in ways we must transform ourselves in order to hear. Thus, the book ends with Morales Bermúdez's narrator-protagonist channeling a prophesy of San Miguel, his town's patron saint:

The night is still walking. Still. There is still the time for suffering. But there is a time that will come to be, when it will be that the people will begin to grow, to come into their own. As if it were the resurrection of Mister Saint Jesus Christ right now. In this same way we will have our resurrection as a people. Our resurrection. At dawn. Under a new sun. In the early morning is how it will be. Early morning. All together we will be rising up. Together. We will bring sticks and hoes. As when it dawns. Just as we do when we go to our milpas. That will be the moment when we rise up; how it is and will be when we break our chains; when it will happen it will be like this. Under a new sun. Then, this time, then, there will be great songs of joy, songs of freedom. With guitar, with drums. With drums. Early in the morning, in the early dawn. That's how it will be. And it will be. All together. Under a new sun. Under a new sun. (185–86)

Bearing Witness to Ethnocide and Femicide among the Lacandón Maya

In *Entre anhelos y recuerdos* (1997), the late Franco-Mexican anthropologist Marie-Odile Marion presents the gripping, tragic tales of six Lacandon Mayan women. She culled these testimonios from her field notes and tape-recorded oral accounts gathered while she conducted fieldwork for her doctoral dissertation, published as *El poder de las hijas de la luna* (1999). These women's tales are interwoven with her own first-person reflections on her experience as an ethnographer and a non-Mayan woman living on and off among the Lacandones for nearly two decades. A complex intersubjectivity haunts this work, as Marion's reflections on her relationships with her interlocutors are interwoven with the women's recollections of the ravages of disease, population reduction, migration, and violence on communal village life. These women's stories present us with a violent account of indigenous assimilation into modern Mexico, illustrating what the women speaking through this text have lost as their communities and natural environments are coercively ushered across the threshold from traditional village life to national and global circuits of economic, political, and religious power.

Entre anhelos y recuerdos stands out not only for its subversion of the indigenista paradigm of benign acculturation into modern national society, but also for its radical critique of traditional fieldwork and research writing methods. This ambivalence toward ethnography's claim to scientific objectivity is evident in passages such as the following, where Marion describes her relationships with the Lacandon women in terms of complicity and conviviality, likening them to interlocutors rather than informants: "for the first time in my life as an ethnologist I had the sensation of being part of their history. I joined them, then, along the paths reaching back into their past, and I found myself emotionally entangled in the hidden nodes of their existence" (90).

The women tell of the sudden and unrelenting incursion into their rainforest communities on the banks of the Lacanjá River in the second half of the twentieth century. Roads are built connecting the jungle to the world through the tourist haunt of Palenque, bringing disease, sexual predator-tourists with "jungle fever" and a foreign (capitalist and patriarchal) system of familial relations whereby women are shunned by their fathers, sons, and husbands, particularly as they age. Practically overnight, streams of white, mestizo, and highland Mayan Indians seeking to extract their fortunes from the jungle's riches—as well as protestant evangelists seeking to alter traditional religious life and suppress polygamy—build inroads into their villages. The newcomers bring money, alcohol, firearms, trinkets, as well as new diseases from the mysterious world of the *dzules* (non-Lacandones). They take precious woods, minerals, and animal skins, leaving behind trails of destruction in the delicate rainforest habitat. As they introduce a commercial economy, they lure Lacandon men away from their communities, fragmenting traditional kinship networks and leaving women, particularly older women, without food and shelter.

In her interpretation of these tales of marginalization, displacement, exile, and loss, Marion seeks to use ethnography to expose the ethnocide in the Lacandón jungle, while at the same time critiquing the discipline for its complicity with that ethnocide. In the introduction, Marion justifies her use of ethnographic fieldwork to critique anthropology's claim to scientific truth and objectivity. At the same time, she warns against the tendency among postmodern ethnographers to fall into an excess of self-reflection and romanticizing of the subjects of their ethnographies. Here, Marion contemplates what she calls the problem of the *firma*, which we can translate as both "signature" and "authorship" :

> The problem of the signature, as the ethnographer must confront it, or as it confronts the ethnographer, demands at once the Olympic attitude of the non-authorial physicist and the sovereign self-consciousness of the hyper-authorial novelist; and it is not permitted to fall into either of these extremes. The first could provoke accusations of insensitivity, of treating people like objects, of hearing the lyrics but not the music, and of course, of ethnocentrism. The second provokes accusations of impressionism, of treating people like puppets, of hearing music that doesn't exist, and of course, of ethnocentrism. (9)

She contends that the scientific pretension to understand alterity is a dense jungle, where the distinction between self and other recedes, precisely because alterity is constructed in the process of signaling it as alterity. In this text, Marion narrates her experience of "interpersonal complicity between anthropologist and her interlocutors" in the context of living together and struggling for mutual understanding. According to Marion, the ethical problems of divulging the communication that takes place in these intimate encounters arise when we consider "where the right to speak begins and where the right to be silent ends" (174). Her words caution that indeed testimonio is not a new, postmodern form of ethnography or of literature but a vital form of resistance and denunciation of injustice. In the epilogue, Marion tells how, back in Mexico City, she read in *La Jornada* the tragic story of a prepubescent Lacandon girl killed at the hands of a gringo photographer who had taken her as his wife. As Marion explains, the girl was "savagely assassinated, bludgeoned to death by her 'husband,' who broke her spinal vertebrae." On her last fieldwork expedition, it had been common knowledge among the families Marion frequented that he routinely beat his young wife. The Lacandon women's testimonios become Marion's confession as she struggles to come to terms with what has happened in her absence, what she did not or could not do to prevent the girl's death. She ends this text with a solemn plea to anthropologists to take their cue from the journalists who work to expose crimes against humanity.

Zapatismo and Cultural Insurgency

In what has been considered the first postmodern conflict of the twentieth century, on January 1, 1994, just as the North American Free Trade Agreement (NAFTA) between the United States, Mexico, and Canada went into effect, a poorly armed but savvy group of Mayan peasants calling themselves the Zapatista Army of National Liberation (EZLN), silently moved out of their jungle training camps to declare war on the Mexican government of then President Carlos Salinas de Gortari. Among other demands, they affirmed their collective rights to political, economic, and cultural self-determination. Citing article 39 of the constitution in their now-famous "Declaration of the Lacandón Jungle," they reminded Mexicans that "national sovereignty resides, essentially and originally, in the people. All public power emanates from the people, and is constituted for the benefit of the same."

Continuing to cite the constitution, the rebels insisted that "the people have, at all times, the inalienable right to alter or modify the form of their government." Because they had made their demands and grievances widely available to an international public by strategically faxing and then posting them on the internet at the precise moment in which they descended upon the provincial cities of San Cristóbal de las Casas, Las Margaritas, Ocosingo, and Altamirano, the Salinas administration found it diplomatically impossible to order the National Army to crush them with military force. The Zapatista rebellion had instantly captured the international left's attention and garnered support from progressive national and international organizations. The Salinas administration, followed by that of Ernesto Zedillo, proceeded to quietly build up its military and paramilitary presence in the southeastern state. The government publicly discredited the movement by branding the charismatic non-indigenous spokesperson, subcomandante Insurgente Marcos, as a manipulator of guileless indigenous peasants. Televisa and TV Azteca blared that outside agitators were using the Indians for their own political ends. This perspective, expressed by political pundits who assumed that the main insurgents were not Indians at all, but rather urban guerrillas, is symptomatic of the indigenista cultural imagination we have examined throughout this book; within this framework, indigenous peoples simply do not have a role in interpreting or shaping their own positions within Mexican society.

Indeed the profusion of letters and communiqués flowing from Marcos's keyboard to the editorial pages of national and international newspapers and websites was not the work of a solitary mind. Rather, it is the collaborative testimonial product of brainstorming between Marcos and his indigenous comrades; this transcultural writing, infused with the syntactical structures and literary devices of indigenous oral traditions, is deployed to effect radical social change. On this battlefield—at once virtual and real—art and politics have proven themselves to be inseparable facets of struggle. At the same time, Marcos's letters and communiqués cannot simply be taken at face value, but instead must be read as literary texts, part of his self-representation as a quixotic *man out of time*. As a self-proclaimed "translator for a revolution," he parodies messianic indigenistas of decades past, calling attention to the absurdity of a society that does not listen to indigenous peoples' voices on their own terms.

For the EZLN, language and culture, symbols and pageantry, had become weapons more powerful, more seductive perhaps than bullets and tanks. Thus, on February 14, 1994, Marcos wrote, or took dictation:

> The oldest of the old of our peoples spoke words to us, words that came from very far away, about when our lives were not, about when our voice was silenced. And the truth journeyed in the words of the oldest of the old of our peoples. And we learned through the words of the oldest of the old that the long night of pain of our people came from the hands and words of the powerful, that our misery was wealth for a few, that on the bones and the dust of our ancestors and our children, the powerful built themselves a house, and that in that house our feet could not enter, and that the light that lit it fed itself on the darkness of our houses, and that its abundant table filled itself on the emptiness of our stomachs, and that their luxuries were born of our misery.[6]

While Marcos insists that he takes orders from his non-Spanish speaking indigenous commanders, and is more of a translator or an "intercultural interpreter" (Lienhard, 1991) than a military leader, the fact that the government has sought to quell the EZLN movement by attempting to buy or kill him off is indicative of persistence of a mainstream discourse of indigenismo, in which the categories *intellectual* and *indigenous* have been made to appear mutually exclusive. Ironically, Marcos's protagonism in the Zapatista struggle has itself served to reinforce this notion that indigenous peoples cannot speak truth to power, but must rely on a non-indigenous interlocutor to do so.

As we have seen throughout this book, complex forces account for the persistence of non-indigenous writers, artists, actors, film directors, and cultural critics as the virtually exclusive channels through which indigenous identity has been articulated throughout much of the twentieth century in Mexico. Cultural production regarding the place and power of indigenous identity has formed part of what Roger Bartra has termed "the imaginary networks of political power"[7] that have buttressed the power of post-revolutionary ruling elites.

The government immediately discredited the Zapatistas and their non-indigenous spokesperson as illegitimate combatants, citing the fact that they hid their faces behind ski masks. This refusal to see the indigenous content and origins of the uprising, as well as the preoccupation with Marcos's role as mediator, are the product of an anachronistic and one-dimensional vision of the indigenous peoples of Chiapas and of Mexico. The Zapatistas offered a belligerent critique of the neoliberal model as well as the colonial legacies that had placed them in the role of an inferior caste for over five hundred years. They asserted that the search for a peaceful resolution to the conflict in Chiapas and for an end to the hegemonic discourse of race in Mexico must begin by recognizing that indigenous peoples are the protagonists, storytellers, artists, and artisans of their own history. In his essay "La Treceava Estela" subcomandante Marcos announces the death of the Zapatista Army and the birth of the Caracoles, or autonomous Zapatista communities. Marcos writes of this transformation and what it has come to mean to be indigenous in Mexico:

> Come. Sit with me a while and let me tell you. We are in rebel lands, lands where the so-called "Zapatistas" live and fight. . . . They are Indian rebels. So they break with the traditional scheme imposed on them from Europe and then from all those that dress in the color of money that dictates how to look and how to be looked upon. Here we have neither the "diabolical" image of a people engaged in human sacrifice to placate the gods, nor the image of the needy Indian with hand outstretched waiting for a handout from those who already have everything, nor of the noble savage perverted by modernity, nor of the child who entertains his folks with his baby-talk, nor the

submissive peon of each and every hacienda that lacerates the history of Mexico, nor of the skillful craftsman whose product is destined to adorn the walls of others who despise him, nor of the ignorant being unable to have an opinion about things far beyond the limited horizon of his geography, nor of a being living in fear of celestial or earthly gods.

The Paradox and Promise of Indigenous Testimonio

Unlike traditional or canonical historical, literary, or social scientific discourse, each of these indigenous testimonios considers subaltern or marginalized people as legitimate agents and communicators of historical processes. According to John Beverley, the emergence of testimonio is tentative proof that third-world writing (particularly in Latin America) has begun a process of emancipation from the bourgeois humanist tradition of literature. But, he cautions, "even while testimonio clearly situates itself against modernist literary models that are based on a subversion or rejection of narratives of identity, it is not an autonomous or 'authentic' form of subaltern culture." Beverley continues:

> Like its ancestor, the picaresque novel, testimonio is a *transitional* cultural form appropriate to processes of social upheaval, but also destined to give way to different forms of representation as these processes move to other stages and the human collectivities that are their agents come into possession of (or lose) new forms of power and knowledge.[8]

Testimonio presents us with a paradox: it undermines the distinction between writing subject, *recopilante*, and referent or object of representation, *testimoniante;* at the same time, it reinscribes that distinction by giving the non-indigenous writer primacy as mastermind or creator of the text. This contradiction leads to the varied forms through which testimonios are gathered and rendered in order to preserve their political relevance and give primacy to the speakers' perspectives, rather than simply reinscribing the well-worn perspectives of dominant society. This rearticulation of authorship and authority mirrors the utopian promise held out by testimonio: the abolition of the power imbalance between writer and speaker, or between social actors who either have or do not have access to mainstream circuits of cultural and political representation.

Indigenismo has been losing ground as a hegemonic discourse of race since the 1970s, in large part because increased state repression and manipulation have eroded its moral veneer of enlightened and peaceful cultural assimilation. These indigenous testimonios reveal that impasse between the post-revolutionary government's idea of the Indian as remote and passive and indigenous peasants' unresolved aspirations for land, liberty, and dignity. Each testimonio constructs a bridge over which each author may cross to escape an ethnocentric epistemology and find another way of imagining the world, to slip into another skin and become a master storyteller by becoming a master listener. Unlike the ethnographic coming-of-age stories discussed in the previous chapter, these indigenous testimonios are constructed with an unmistakable attention to the seams, discontinuities, and lacunae in the translation of spoken raw material into written text.

As they transcribe, translate, and editorialize on the thoughts and actions of their indigenous interlocutors, these writers have created a radical break with the romantic yet abject depictions of indigenous life and consciousness found in indigenista literary and ethnographic works. Their work anticipates a new type of cultural formation, one in which the discourse of mestizaje as racial and cultural absorption of indigenous culture into Hispanic culture is replaced with that of pluriculturalism and the acknowledgment of indigenous people as subjects of their own histories rather than objects of academic and political projects. Whereas indigenista literary and ethnographic narratives hold out the promise of equality and justice through acculturation to a national mestizo family, in these indigenous testimonios, the threshold of belonging is reversed. The question is no longer how to help integrate indigenous people into national society. These testimonios document indigenous peoples' struggles for autonomy and cultural renewal in the face of accelerated internal and transnational colonialism. Perhaps these are the foundational narratives for the imagined community the Zapatistas call civil society, as they construct and mirror the promises and pitfalls of intercultural communication and solidarity in this new millennium.

From Malinche to Matriarchal Utopia

Gendered and Sexualized Visions of Indigeneity

This chapter examines some of the dominant representations of indigeneity and national identity we have seen throughout this book in order to show how they coalesce with ideologies of gender and sexuality in contemporary Mexico. In particular, I look at how these ideologies are currently being challenged within new social movements led by indigenous women. I examine representations of women and muxes in the Isthmus of Tehuantepec, Oaxaca, alongside modern representations of Malinche, Cortés's translator and consort in the sixteenth-century conquest of Mexico. While both have become icons of indigenous femininity, Isthmus Zapotec women are represented as matriarchal and powerful while Malinche is fashioned as subjugated yet manipulative. Examined together, these two myths born of post-revolutionary cultural nationalism can tell us a great deal about the intersections of race, gender, and sexuality in the Mexican cultural imagination. In turn, they can help us understand indigenous women's movements as a challenge to these hegemonic identity constructions.

In *Blossoms of Fire* (2000), directed by Maureen Gosling, the narrator tells us "'Mexico's matriarchy' is what they call Juchitán, a city in the Isthmus of Tehuantepec. It's a place where women light up the streets like flowers; but if you cross them, they'll cuss you out." In this film, Gosling sets out to discover how this Zapotec region of Oaxaca has gained a reputation over the centuries as an unabashedly welcoming place to grow up gay or transgendered (*muxe* for a gay or woman-identified man and *nguiu* for a lesbian or butch woman in Zapotec), a place where women are visible and vocal

Women bearing gifts at a *vela*. (From *Blossoms of Fire*, 2000. Reproduced by permission from Gosling, fig. 1)

within the most public spheres of society, and at the same time, a place synonymous with grassroots political struggle. Outsiders are drawn to the Juchitecas' elaborate blouses, flowing skirts, ample bodies, and the dignified way that women (and men dressed as women) move through space with something Isthmus Zapotecs refer to as *gracia* (grace) and *presencia* (presence).

Non-Zapotec artists and writers have often celebrated Zapotec women of the Isthmus of Tehuantepec, and most notably of the market city of Juchitán, as paragons of Mexican female beauty and independence. To get a sense of the sultry naturalism that infuses these iconic visions of Isthmus Zapotec femininity, we can draw upon many sources: for example, Sergei Eisenstein's classic unfinished film *¡Que viva México!*; Elena Poniatowska's travel essay "Juchitán de las mujeres"; Miguel Covarrubias's travelogues and paintings; Diego Rivera's and Frida Kahlo's paintings; as well as Tina Modotti's and Graciela Iturbide's photographs. These varied works all have fueled the enticing myth of a matriarchal utopia by portraying a lush southerly enclave with a proud monopoly on an exuberantly feminine and independent existence.

While these representations celebrate Isthmus Zapotec women for their charisma and self-reliance, they have also spawned myths about Isthmus Zapotec sexuality and social behavior that seem degrading. In *Blossoms of Fire*, Istmeños show the viewer that these representations are untrue. As a challenge to the stylized images created by non-Zapotecs, we find the works of Isthmus Zapotec writers and artists—among them Manuel López Chiñas, Victor de la Cruz, and Francisco Toledo—engaging playfully (or scornfully) the wanton gaze of outside observers. In fact, several generations of Isthmus Zapotec artists, writers, musicians, and cultural critics have gained a measure of national and international recognition perhaps unmatched by that of any other indigenous group in Mexico. According to Marinella Miano Borruso (2002, 96), since the late Andrés Henestrosa first led the Academy of the Zapotec Language and the New Society of Juchitec Students in the 1930s, Isthmus Zapotec artists and writers have worked to affirm cultural pluralism in Mexico, refusing to let their regional particularities be absorbed by the homogenizing ideal of mestizo nationalist political and cultural subjectivity promoted by post-revolutionary elites.[1]

Using the documentary film *Blossoms of Fire* as my primary source for analysis, in the first part of this chapter I examine the ways in which Isthmus Zapotecs playfully deconstruct and reconfigure the myths created about them by outsiders. The portrait that emerges is that of a society in which socially coherent configurations of sex, gender, desire, and social relations exist comfortably outside what Judith Butler refers to as the "heterosexual matrix" (1990, xxviii). From the film's extensive interviews and scenes of daily life with gay, lesbian, and transgendered Juchitecos and their families, we can appreciate that what is normative in terms of gender and sexuality in the Isthmus is not necessarily *heteronormative*. I explore relationships among the following three elements: the valorization of women in their different roles as breadwinners, family members, and transmitters of culture; the capacity for Istmeños to resist the pressures of outside domination, specifically since recent free-trade initiatives have set transnational developers' sights on the region; and finally, the multiple options available for socially coherent gender and sexual identities within family and community. I find that the representations of Isthmus Zapotec women as savvy entrepreneurs and respected community leaders in this film provide an inspiring contrast to the ways in which women's economic and sociopolitical agency have been consistently euphemized and made invisible within mainstream discussions of national identity and political imperatives in Mexico.[2]

My second concern—and the one that is critical to this book's analysis of the cultural politics of ethnic identities in contemporary Mexico—is with what might be gained or lost if we buy into the idea of an alluring gynocentric paradise in the Isthmus of Tehuantepec. To what rule, exactly, are Isthmus Zapotecs considered the exception? What might these images of gender and sexual freedom limited to one specific corner of Mexico tell us about how national identity has been imagined—gendered, sexualized, and racialized—within the wider field of Mexican visual and literary production?

The vivacious image of an empowering, woman-centered culture among Isthmus Zapotecs that seduces the viewer of *Blossoms of Fire* contrasts deeply with the central metaphors with which cultural nationalists have constructed the foundational myths of modern Mexican gender and racial identity. I am referring specifically to the myth of a passive, pliant, indigenous femininity embodied in the historical figure of la Malinche. Malinche, more affectionately known as Malintzin, Malinalli, or doña Marina, was Hernán Cortés's translator, intercultural interpreter, and mother to his child, and has been symbolically assigned the role of scorned and abject mother of the Mexican people.[3] Like the biblical Eve, Malinche is the scapegoat, the ambivalent accomplice who "opened" Mexico to conquest and subjugation. Central motifs in the writings of Octavio Paz and Carlos Fuentes as well as the murals of Rivera and of José Clemente Orozco focus on the image of Malinche as an object of pity and rage, *la chingada madre*, the raped Indian mother with downcast eyes and restrained body, and Cortés as the domineering and scornful European father, *el chingón*.

Here I will focus specifically on Orozco's 1926 mural titled *Cortés and Malinche* and Paz's essay "Sons of Malinche" from his 1950 *Labyrinth of Solitde*. With these and other examples, I aim to highlight the ways in which artists and writers who were associated with national popular state formation following the Revolution of 1910 have considered their national identity to stem from a gendered mestizaje—that is to say, from the genetic and cultural mixture and absorption of (female) indigenous traits into (male) Euro-Iberian ones.

Thus, this notion of a matriarchal utopia, of powerful Indian women who, as Elena Poniatowska describes them, "walk like towers" (1993, 82) and are "very proud to be women" (1993, 77), presents us with an appealing counter-narrative to the disempowering mother-whore myth of Malinche. The question I seek to answer is not whether Isthmus Zapotec society is matriarchal or not. Rather, I ask whether this notion, by projecting an image of indigenous women's empowerment onto one specific region, may legitimize dominant discourses that imagine Mexican women, and indigenous women in particular, as passive and powerless yet paradoxically self-serving

Mayordomos at a vela in San Blas Atempa. (*From Blossoms of Fire*, 2000. Reproduced by permission from Gosling, fig. 2)

and treacherous. The urgent question here then becomes: is our ability to take note of indigenous women's social agency in regions of Mexico other than the Isthmus of Tehuantepec foreclosed by nationalist myths that equate femininity and indigeneity with resigned acceptance of domination?

I would like to suggest that the myth of Isthmus Zapotec society as a matriarchal utopia may indeed be appropriated as a strategy of containment, as the proverbial "exception that proves the rule" when seen through a romantic lens. However, I also wonder about the possibility of accessing this mythology beyond the region. I suggest that it can help us to see past the binaries of masculine and feminine, modernity and tradition, productive male labor and reproductive female labor, and public and domestic realms of life in order to understand how gender and sexual identities are actually lived and imagined in Mexico.

Fact from Fantasy: Engendering the City of Women

As we hear in the opening segment of *Blossoms of Fire*, NPR reporter Katie Davis proclaims that "the women of Juchitán work, drink beer, dance, and make love all in a day. Then they get up at dawn and do it again. And do it again and again. That's the way things have always been in Juchitán, Oaxaca." As Gosling narrates, her task of sifting out fact from fantasy is further complicated when the week she begins filming a scandal breaks out involving the foreign media: as the Juchitecs interviewed in *Blossoms* tell it, the fashion magazine *Elle* has recently published an article depicting the women of Juchitán as oversexed, carousing bullies who pay young lovers and prostitute themselves while their meek husbands have to beg for beer money.

Yet the *Elle* article and the NPR segment are only the most exaggerated among a slew of instances in which travelers, journalists, artists, and writers have found in the Isthmus an ideal location onto which they might project their own longings for a space outside the confines of patriarchal domination and capitalist alienation. In the 1930s, Sergei Eisenstein depicted Juchitán as a proto-socialist, erotic utopia in his classic film ¡*Que viva México!* While the camera lingers on sensual bathers frolicking in a river, Eisenstein muses, "You are pursued by the idea that Eden was not located between the Tigris and the Euphrates, but here, between the Gulf of Mexico and Tehuantepec." Eisenstein's magical realist aesthetic playfully draws on Rivera's early paintings of bathing Isthmus maidens with pendulous breasts as well as Kahlo's defiant self-portraits in traditional Tehuana matrimonial dress. Iturbide's exotic photographs of Zapotec women compose yet another surreal archive of a woman-centered spirituality and poetics of daily life. Her photographs echo these previous images of Juchitán as a land of abundance and leisure. These visions of a land and people outside history draw mimetic relationships between animals and humans, between the rhythms of the natural world and those of people. They suggest that the bounty of the sea, the fertility of the soil, and the electricity in the relentless warm breezes all contribute to the unique sensuality of Isthmus culture. In Eisenstein's film, the flirtatious rituals of parrots and monkeys are juxtaposed with scenes of young lovers anticipating their honeymoon. In Iturbide's photos, Juchitec goddesses strike provocative poses with iguanas and fish, organic extensions of their own bodies.

Poniatowska's titillating travel essay, "Juchitán de las mujeres," which includes a photo-essay by Iturbide in the collection *Luz y luna, las lunitas* (Poniatowska, 1994), further mythologizes the region as a languid and lusty garden of earthly delights, where public space, economic exchange, and erotic humor are exclusively feminine domains. "Man is a kitten between their legs, a puppy they have to admonish, 'Stay there'" (Poniatowska, 1993, 133).[4] Poniatowska breathlessly speculates on the "unending sexual activity" of the Juchitecs, which she suggests is inspired by the howling of cats, dogs, mares, and every type of wild animal in heat. "The he-turtles come to spend themselves on the she-turtles; they make love until death finds them. . . . Juchitán is in heat all year long. . . . The wind spreads ocean musk upon the land of Juchitán, musk that inflames desire. And hope" (Poniatowska, 1994, 95).

For Poniatowska, Juchitán is "not like any other town," not only because it presented the first and only successful challenge to single party rule by the PRI (Institutional Revolutionary Party) throughout its nearly seventy-year governance, but because women literally *own* the streets and their own bodies:

> You should see them arrive like walking towers, their windows open, their heart like a window, their nocturnal girth visited by the moon. You should see them arrive; they already are the government, they, the people, guardians of men, distributors of food, their children riding astride their hips or lying in the hammocks of their breasts, the wind in their skirts, flowered vessels, the honeycomb of their sex overflowing with men. Here they come shaking their wombs, pulling the *machos* toward them, the machos who, in contrast with them, wear light colored pants, shirts, leather sandals, and palm hats, which they lift high in the air as they shout, "Long live Juchitec women!" (Poniatowska, 1993, 133–34)

Many other artistic, literary, and mass media approaches to Isthmus Zapotec culture envision it as a matriarchal society; yet in doing so they define matriarchy as a simple inversion of patriarchal domination, painting a picture of Isthmus Zapotec women as brawny Amazons who lord it over meek and subservient men. *Blossoms of Fire* departs from previous treatments by pointing to the abyss between sex and gender, refusing to go along with those who would see the world in terms of some kind of "–archy" (patriarchy, matriarchy, or otherwise). Instead, it reaches beyond these binary oppositions that conflate male and female with dominant and subjugated, active and passive, modern and traditional, public and domestic, productive and reproductive labor to focus on traditional Zapotec gender roles as they are locally understood.

The question "why do women seem so powerful here?" is posed at the outset of the documentary. *Blossoms of Fire* leads us to conclude that the answer is not to be found in some spiritual essence or environmental determinism, but rather in the material base of Isthmus Zapotec culture as it has developed and changed over time. Gosling observes that traditional gender-specific roles dictate that women be entrepreneurs, managing community and household affairs while the men carry out the behind-the-scenes labor in the fields and at sea as fishermen. Through conversations with men and women, the viewer gets the sense that public and private realms are certainly "gendered," such that men and women perform distinct sets of tasks. Juchitec sociologist Marina Menenses (1997) contrasts Isthmus Zapotec notions of gender complementarity with Euro-American feminism's emphasis on gender equality.

The difference, she explains, is that the tasks men and women perform are considered equally valuable within society, providing both with income, prestige, and independence. Yet from the vantage point of the central market, what Gosling calls the "pulsing heart of the local economy," which dominates the main square and spills out onto side streets, these realms do not appear to be gendered in quite the same way as in Euro-American or "Western" social practices. Women are associated with money, with public space, with community planning, and with Zapotec cultural autonomy. Within this apparently rigid separation of gender domains, however, it is understood that male and female children will grow up to define their own gender roles in keeping with their unique desires and aptitudes.

Hence, the second major question this film poses, regarding the social position of gays and lesbians, proves to be intimately related to the question of feminine empowerment, namely how does one account for the relative openness about lesbian, gay, and transgendered social identities in the Isthmus? Many of the men and women interviewed in *Blossoms of Fire*, and others with whom I have spoken, draw connections between the central roles that women play in public spheres and the Isthmus Zapotec tradition of openness about non-heterosexual social identities. In the film, Vicky affirms "lesbianism is something one is born with." She says that unlike in Mexico City or the United States, there is no such thing as "coming out" in the Isthmus. "When did I realize I was gay? . . . as soon as I realized I exist in the world," remarks Manuel. Vicky suggests that since identifying oneself as gay or lesbian does not imply an alteration in one's potential status in the social structure, non-heterosexual social identities do not carry the same stigma or connotations of shame as in other cultures. Being gay or lesbian is not considered a threat to community or family cohesiveness; it is a matter of reconsidering how household and community duties will be taken care of effectively.

In *Blossoms of Fire*, the community's struggles for political autonomy are linked to traditional gender roles and sexual norms, even if these roles and norms might not appear traditional to outside observers. There are some notable ways in which gender might actually be a more fluid notion in the Isthmus; the Juchitecs who reflect on their lives in this film emphasize that gender identification stems from *oficio*, that is to say, from the work roles with which one is associated rather than from real or perceived sexual preference.

One scene from the film illustrates this point well: Felina, a sought-after beautician, seamstress, and paragon of fashion, sits with her mother and father near the family's cornfield, striking coy poses as her father despondently reflects on his son's position within the family. With resignation he concludes that "if he were not muxe, he would be here, helping me with my work, but what can I do, this is the way he was born." Felina's mother, on the other hand, smiles indulgently, with the knowing satisfaction that her son provides income for the family and companionship for her in her domestic activities.

In my own travels in Juchitán, I met a couple who had been married for forty-seven years, Catalina and Eusebio (not their real names). I talked with Catalina as she lay in her hammock, weak and in pain from cancer. She told me that, like many older women in Juchitán today, she takes great pride in having worked hard, managed her income well, and financed her five children's university educations. Eusebio ceased his sweeping to join our conversation, gesturing toward the broom and explaining with a tender smile that since his wife had become ill, he had become muxe. By this it was clear that for him being muxe had more to do with the kind of work he was engaged in than with sexual identity. To be muxe, a femme, is to be keeper of the house, he implied. These examples illustrate that individuals arrive at gendered identities by performing certain tasks and only secondarily by outward appearance or sexual identification.

The Isthmus Zapotecs featured in this film also link their current struggles for self-determination in the face of transnational investments in the region to their long history of fending off Aztecs, Spaniards, the French, and the Mexican government. As Gosling describes the current situation, "the Isthmus region's strategic location between the Gulf of Mexico and the Pacific, along with its significant oil reserves, makes this area very attractive to investors. Now, massive development projects threaten to alter the way of life here."

At the same time, the wry editing, which creates some poetic juxtapositions and subtly divergent points of view, allows the viewer to construct an image of Isthmus culture that is far from static, hermetic, or idealized. Instead, the viewer is able to appreciate the ways in which social identities are dynamically constructed and concepts of tradition and social mores are not necessarily conservative or heterosexist. The film thus concludes that

Manuel embroiders. (From *Blossoms of Fire*, 2000. Reproduced by permission from Gosling, fig. 3)

the search for an island of cultural authenticity in the Isthmus is a search that is bound to lead to yet more fantasy and projection.

Malinche, the Conquerable Sign

Ironically, the notion of a powerful and erotic feminine essence in the Isthmus of Tehuantepec and that of Malinche as raped and humiliated mother of the Mexican people both have their roots in post-revolutionary nationalist culture. By juxtaposing these two myths, we can begin to see the fissure between indigenous identities and how they are fabricated in the indigenista cultural imagination.

According to Estela Serret, the emergence of a cohesive state-directed discourse of national identity in Mexico stems from two interrelated historical factors: "the triumph of the political project which grew out of the Mexican Revolution and the political, economic, and ideological cohesion of the Mexican nation-state" (1999, 256). As was discussed in chapter one, within the circuits of visual and literary production patronized by post-revolutionary state institutions, the figure of the mestizo is crafted as the symbol of national unity and as the privileged referent in the construction of political and cultural subjectivity. It is through this privileging of cultural homogeneity, of assimilation of the feminine to the masculine, the indigenous to the Hispanic, and the traditional to the modern that the historical figures of Malinche and Cortés are recast as mythical mother and father. As Cortés's translator and consort, Malinche has been invoked by practitioners of mestizo nationalist ideology as the archetypal abject Indian mother of mestizo national identity and used to legitimize the subaltern status of indigenous women in Mexican society.

Natividad Gutiérrez (1999) provides a compelling description of the ambivalence with which intellectuals and policy makers have endeavored to construct a culturally and linguistically uniform nation. While they trace the origin of the nation to the indigenous past, they also foster centralized cultural and social institutions aimed to integrate indigenous peoples into the mainstream of the nation. According to Gutiérrez, one of the major ethnic myths of national integration is that of common descent, which constructs the figure of Malinche as the mother of the Mexican people, thereby creating the illusion of a homogenous collective indigenous identity, clearly gendered female, that fuses romantically with an equally homogenous collective Spanish identity construed as masculine. This fictitious genealogy, she argues, is reinforced through standardized primary public school textbooks that teach children that Malinche gave birth to the nation. According to Gutiérrez, this foundational myth has far-reaching effects on contemporary political rhetoric: "In Mexico the symbolic creation attributed to Malinche—the mestizo race—still plays a key ideological role in modern politics; politicians believe that mestizaje is the 'antithesis of racist discourses and it has the capacity to incorporate differences and to reject racial puritanisms'" (1999, 149).

However, in Mexico's current political climate, mestizo nationalism as an ideology capable of shaping social imperatives is clearly at an impasse. Two interrelated factors have rendered this ideology anachronistic in times of globalization: first, the emergence in recent decades of indigenous movements for autonomy have put pressure on the state to both recognize Mexico as a multiethnic nation and grant collective rights to indigenous communities; and second, the federal government has dismantled its populist economic and social development model in favor of an export-oriented, social austerity model as a means of reducing the mountains of foreign debt the nation has incurred over the past four decades. The bottom line here is that even as women's economic burdens have shifted in these times, such that work outside the home is no longer an option but an imperative, mainstream representations of women's social roles have remained anchored in the narratives of mestizo nationalism. Since indigenous women especially face a double negation of their economic and socio-political agency, it is important to look again at the myth of Isthmus Zapotec exceptionality, this time using the myth to question the ways in which our understandings of gender and ethnic identity have been imagined within nationalist cultural configurations that equate *mexicanidad* or Mexican identity with mestizaje.

In *Labyrinth of Solitude* (1985), for example, Paz sketches a portrait of indigeneity as not only poor and marginalized from modern national life but also as truly *other* in both a spiritual and a physical sense:

> The otherness eludes the notions of poverty and wealth, development or backwardness: it is a complex of unconscious attitudes and structures which, far from being survivals from an extinct world, are vital, constituent parts of our contemporary culture. The other Mexico, the submerged and repressed, reappears in the modern Mexico: when we talk with ourselves, we talk with it; when we talk with it, we talk with ourselves. . . . By it, I mean that gaseous reality formed by the beliefs, fragments of beliefs, images and concepts which history deposits in the subsoil of the social psyche, that cave or cellar in continuous somnolence and likewise in perpetual fermentation. (287)

For Paz, indigenous marginalization is not considered to stem from institutionalized structures of inequality, "poverty and wealth," but rather from intractable cultural differences. Paz describes "Indianness" as a central though disembodied part of the Mexican social psyche, an absent presence or ambivalent agency that conjures up the figure of Malinche. Paz constructs indigeneity as an aesthetic and spiritual underground stream, the feminized other through which the modern (non-indigenous or de-Indianized) masculine self is articulated as the subject of national identity.

This vision of Mexican identity as a gendered binary of indigenous and Hispanic elements is not unique to Paz. It echoes the sentiments of José Vasconcelos, the architect of Mexico's post-revolutionary public education system and author of the influential essay *The Cosmic Race*, who trumpeted that: "We are Indian, blood and soil: the language and civilization are Spanish" ([1925] 1997, 37). For Vasconcelos as for Paz, indigeneity is equated with the earth, the lower body, the semiotic, embryonic, unformed, primordial, feminine, and irrational; conversely, the Hispanic element of Mexico is equated with the universal, the upper body, the semantic, the adult, the civilized, evolved, masculine, and rational. Just as patriarchal discourse deems *woman* a collective singular noun—an empty vessel or an empty signifier and therefore a site for multiple and conflicting articulations—here the indigenous *other* is assigned a similarly passive role, as cultural raw material whose being and meaning surface only when articulated through Hispanic subjectivity. Bartolomé Alonso Camaal, a Yucatec Maya teacher and civil servant, puts it bluntly when he states, "When Indian knowledge is appropriated, it is called mestizaje" (quoted in Gutiérrez, 1999, 153).

In Paz's assessment, indigeneity is not a sign of backwardness but a "gaseous" collective unconscious, a repressed alter ego that forms the substrate of Mexican identity.[5] Although indigenous peoples, and especially indigenous women, are clearly marginalized from the modern state, mestizo nationalist discourse constructs indigeneity as an abstract entity or essence that forms the dark feminine core of identity in all Mexicans, regardless of whether they have indigenous ancestry or meaningful contact with living indigenous peoples. Thus, in "Sons of Malinche," Paz constructs a metonymic relationship between Malinche and all Mexican women: "In effect, every woman—even when she gives herself willingly— is torn open by the man, is the Chingada. In a certain sense, all of us, by the simple fact of being born of woman, are hijos de la Chingada, sons of Eve. But the singularity of the Mexican resides, I believe, in his violent, sarcastic humiliation of the Mother and his no-less violent affirmation of the Father" (1985, 80).

For Paz, Malinche as reluctant mother of the nation has an alter-ego relationship with the Virgin of Guadalupe, Mexico's revered brown-skinned virgin, also seen as mother of the nation. Within mestizo nationalism, then, feminine identity is codified in and caught between these two figures, one mother who orphans her child because he reminds her of the rape she has suffered, and the other who adopts and consoles the child orphaned by his rejecting mother.

> In contrast to Guadalupe, who is the Virgin Mother, the Chingada is the violated Mother. . . . Guadalupe is pure receptivity and the benefits she bestows are of the same order: she consoles, quiets, dries tears, calms passions. The Chingada is even more passive. Her passivity is abject: she does not resist violence, but is an inert heap of bones, blood, and dust. Her taint is constitutional and resides, as we said earlier, in her sex. This passivity, open to the outside world, causes her to lose her identity: she is the Chingada. She loses her name; she is no one; she disappears into nothingness; she is Nothingness. And yet she is the cruel incarnation of the feminine condition.
>
> If the Chingada is a representation of the violated Mother, it is appropriate to associate her with the Conquest, which was also a violation, not only in the historical sense but also in the very flesh of Indian women. The symbol of this violation is doña Malinche, the mistress of Cortés. It is true that she gave herself voluntarily to the

conquistador, but he forgot her as soon as her usefulness was over. Doña Marina becomes a figure representing the Indian women who were fascinated, violated, or seduced by the Spaniards. And as a small boy will not forgive his mother if she abandons him to search for his father, the Mexican people have not forgiven La Malinche for her betrayal. She embodies the open, the *chingado*, to our closed, stoic, impassive Indians. (1985, 85–86)

For Paz, neither Malinche nor Guadalupe can be a subject of Mexican national identity per se; they can only be conduits for that identity. Together they embody the essential dichotomy between good and bad women that creates the conditions for the Mexican psychic state of solitude. The Mexican condition, he affirms, is centered on this drive to transfer affection from the rejecting biological mother to the adopting, accepting mother, she who is "pure receptivity."

We can see here that mestizo nationalist discourse melds ethnicity and gender; yet equally important is how it functions to edge class identities out of the field of symbols from which national identity is constructed. Manuel Gamio, considered the father of modern Mexican anthropology, set a precedent for the rhetorical conflation of ethnic and class categories when he stated in his influential *Forjando patria* that the mestizo is "the eternal rebel, the traditional enemy of the class of pure blood or foreign blood, the author and director of uprisings and rebellions and the class which has best understood the just lament of the Indian class" ([1916] 1960, 95). For Gamio, mestizo identity is equivalent to class identity, and to be mestizo is to be the revolutionary protagonist of twentieth-century Mexico. Here, Indian identity is also equated with social class, but the active (gendered male) role belongs solely to the mestizo, the author of the nation cast as the ideal mediator between a besieged, feminized Indian class and a predatory "class of pure blood or foreign blood."

According to María Josefina Saldaña-Portillo, Gamio's revolutionary nationalism constitutes a strategy for minority rule, as he casts the Indian as the wellspring of *latent* revolutionary energies and national culture and the mestizo as the national hero capable of channeling and interpreting this raw potential in order to create a mature national culture and national economy. Saldaña-Portillo argues: "By conflating blood with ideas, industries, virtues and vices—the very stuff of culture—Gamio biologizes a cultural metaphor for citizenship in the nation. Only the mestizo is capable of producing a national culture by virtue of his mixed blood, blood that draws him sympathetically toward, though always at a critical remove from, all things Indian and drives him away from all things 'foreign'" (2003, 210).

As Saldaña-Portillo notes, Gamio constructs this Indian difference as a dormant potentiality to be absorbed and refined by the revolutionary mestizo subject. For Gamio, indigeneity is "anachronistic and inappropriate" until it is effectively interpreted by the "class of mixed-blood," and protected from the "class of pure blood or foreign blood" ([1916] 1960, 95). In Gamio's *Forjando patria* as well as Vasconcelos's *The Cosmic Race*, the protagonist, the central historical subject of the newly unshackled nation, is unmistakably mestizo. While the antagonist is the fair-skinned and bloated capitalist, the afflicted yet dignified transitional figure—the element to be incorporated—is the modern-day Indian.

As a "cultural metaphor for citizenship" (Saldaña-Portillo, 2003, 210), then, mestizaje resolves the question of ancestry, of the biological origins of the pueblo by activating the myth of Malinche and Cortés as national mother and father; citizenship is thus gendered at the same time that it is racially codified. The hegemonic relation established through the mestizo-as-citizen formulation locates the drama of national origins at the key site of Spanish conquest as well as the center of post-revolutionary national popular state consolidation, in the metropolis of ancient México-Tenochtitlan and modern-day Mexico City.

As an important element in this project of state consolidation, in the 1920s and 1930s, Vasconcelos and other powerful administrators of the post-revolutionary state commissioned murals by Orozco, Rivera, David Álfaro Siqueiros, and others to inscribe their visions of Mexican history and cultural identity directly onto the urban architecture, and specifically onto the most important government buildings. These artists' representations of indigeneity and of national origins depart from Gamio's and Vasconcelos's formulations in important ways. In the works of Orozco, Siqueiros, and Rivera, the image of the abject and subordinated Indian coexists with the image of the Indian as dignified and self-actualized, often within the same work. Though patronized by the post-revolutionary state to create a uniquely mestizo art for an emerging mestizo nation, these murals display conflicting notions regarding the place and power of indigenous peoples within this emerging post-revolutionary cultural imagination.

These artistic renderings provide material from which we may draw conclusions regarding my second question, which asks what is at stake when Isthmus Zapotec culture is considered anomalous in the context of Mexican national culture. In several murals and paintings by Rivera, Orozco, and others, indigenous figures are portrayed with sealed lips and an enigmatic, impenetrable gaze downward and out into oblivion, a furtive or blind gaze that eschews contact with the viewer. Rendered in earth tones that blend into shadowy backgrounds, indigenous bodies appear formless and flaccid, conveying stillness, silence, and annihilation. Consider these representations in contrast with the bold images of Isthmus Zapotecs, which invariably center upon the piercing gaze of self-assured Indian women!

While Rivera's figure of the Indian appears as an ebulient repository of utopian longings, springing from a dark, rich soil, for Orozco, indigeneity presents the viewer with an image of abject tension, painfully outlined against a parched earth. In contrast with Rivera's deep reds, rich ochres, and mellow brown tones on rounded figures, Orozco's frescoes depict immobile indigenous figures in dismal, monochromatic tones and stark plays of darkness and light, taut and flaccid muscles. The indigenous figures appear rooted to the earth in agonized resignation. Bodies are frozen and crouching in their nakedness, their movement restricted by the bodies of white men.

Of particular interest here is Orozco's fresco *Cortés and Malinche*, painted above a stairwell at the Antiguo Colegio de San Ildefonso in Mexico City. In this fresco Cortés gently squeezes Malinche's right hand in his while he holds his sinewy left arm across her torso, as if to prevent her from using her left hand to touch the dead, emaciated body lying face down at their feet. Desmond Rochfort describes the triangular relationship between Cortés, Malinche, and the figure below in the following terms: "In Orozco's portrayal, the couple are joined (sic) hand in hand in an act of union. This union, however, is seemingly contingent upon Cortez's subjugation of the Indian, represented in the fresco by a prone and naked figure under the Spaniard's right foot. Cortez's left arm both prevents an act of supplication on Malinche's part and acts as a final separation from her former life. The image of Cortés and Malinche symbolizes synthesis, subjugation, and the ambivalence of her position in the story of the nation's history of colonial intervention" (1993, 44–46).

While both seated figures are naked and occupy the same plane, connoting parity between them, the light cast on Cortés's body makes him appear invulnerable, as if he were covered in gleaming armor. With his left knee pressing against her legs, he prevents her from planting her feet firmly on the ground; only her toes anxiously grip the earth. In this position, she cannot move. Although her body is robust and muscular, only the muscles in her neck, face, and toes are active. While she looks down and askance, Cortés keeps a watchful and menacing eye on her. His muscles are taut, his right foot firmly resting on the thin naked figure below. The focal point of the composition is Malinche's breast; while her eyes, dart-

José Clemente Orozco, *Cortés and Malinche*. Mural, 1926.
Escuela Nacional Preparatoria San Ildefonso, Mexico City,
D.F., Mexico (Schalkwijk/Art Resource; reprinted with
permission by Artist's Rights Society)

ing apprehensively under lowered lids, appear to struggle to avoid Cortés's
menacing gaze, her one exposed nipple (the other is covered by Cortés's
arm) stares out at the viewer like a large astonished eye.

In *Franciscan Monk*, also by Orozco, a skeletal indigenous figure kneels
before an enormous friar, who stoops to press his face into him, kissing
him in a stultifying embrace. It is almost as if the friar were strangling
the Indian, whose thin arms are thrown back helplessly. Like Malinche,
he cannot move; his body is both exposed and enclosed by the Friar's suf-
focating grasp. Is he being held up or pushed down to the ground by the

José Clemente Orozco, *Franciscan Monk*. Mural, 1926.
Escuela Nacional Preparatoria San Ildefonso, Mexico City,
D.F., Mexico. (Schalkwijk/Art Resource; reprinted with
permission by Artist's Rights Society)

friar? The closed eyes and deeply furrowed brows of both figures meet
tenderly, symbolizing, in the words of Rochfort, their common humanity; yet the Indian's blurred face, his androgynous naked body—with its
exposed ribs, ankle, and hip bones—contrast with the friar's expressive
facial features and the billowy folds of his cloak, which hangs loosely on
his enormous, energetic frame. Depicted as germinal moments in an endless cycle of dehumanization and redemption, subjugation and salvation,
these frescoes evoke Orozco's ambivalent vision of biological mestizaje
and religious conversion as both inexorable trauma and utopian dream.

This leitmotif of mestizaje as *pharmakos*—as the original problem and the ultimate cure for all that ails modern Mexican society—signals a profound anxiety surrounding the foundational narrative that casts Malinche and Cortés as mother and father of the nation. When we examine this post-revolutionary refashioning of the historical figure of Malinche alongside the myth of matriarchal utopia among Isthmus Zapotecs, we can begin to understand how the latter might function as a safe repository for those heterogeneous, unconquerable elements that threaten the state's limited imaginings of the national body.

Conclusions: Rethinking Indigenous Women's Agency in a Postcolonial Frame

In Mexican visual arts and literature, Zapotec culture in the Isthmus of Tehuantepec has been celebrated as at once a locus of women's social power, a place where homosexuality and transgendering are embraced as integral aspects of society, and finally, a perennial vanguard of grassroots political organizing. These images of indigenous, gay, and women-centered empowerment among Isthmus Zapotecs contrast profoundly with dominant narratives of Mexican national identity. Within these narratives, the figure of Malinche has taken on a notoriety that stretches far beyond her historical role in the sixteenth-century conquest of central Mexico. As Cortés's multilingual interpreter, consul, and mother to his child, Malinche has been invoked in twentieth-century cultural production as the archetypal abject mother of a modern mestizo nation. In locating the origins of modern Mexico in the sexual union of the historical figures of Malinche and Hernán Cortés, mestizo nationalist imaginings negate the multiethnic composition of pre- and post-conquest Mesoamerican society. At the same time, they buttress a series of binary oppositions in which the feminine is associated with indigeneity and subjugation while the masculine is associated with hispanicity and conquest. As an object of scorn, her name, which isn't really even her name, has been invoked to negate the agency of indigenous women in Mexican society. The historical figure of Malinche is conjured up today when one is accused of being a *malinchista*, of selling one's people out to foreign interests, as it implies accepting subaltern status in exchange for a modicum of personal benefit in the context of colonial or neocolonial domination. Yet as Frances Karttunen writes, "This is no love story, no tale of blind ambition and racial betrayal. It is the record of a gifted woman in impossible circumstances carving out survival one day at a time" (1997, 312). Today in Chicana and Mexican feminist thought, Malinche has become a symbol of the postcolonial condition, or, as Gayatri Chakravorty Spivak would have it, of finding oneself in the ambivalent position of having to "critique a space one inhabits intimately" ([1990] 1998, 228). It is not only Malinche's real name and origins that are irretrievable, but more importantly, her agency. Was she raped? Did she willingly participate in the conquest of Mexico? Jean Franco delves into the complexities of how Malinche's elusive agency constitutes the hegemonic relation established through her image:

> As Spivak says: "Neocolonialism is fabricating its allies by proposing a share of the center in a seemingly new way." That is to say, neocolonialism constructs its allies by proposing a new way to participate in the center. In the sixteenth century, participation in the center was sealed by various "contracts" that gave Malinche a letter of inclusion. . . . But as Margo Glanz has aptly noted, Malinche acts in the process of conquest each time she tries to negotiate instead of fight. It is not that Marina "chooses" this option, as Todorov affirms, but that she covered a catachresis brought about by a previous act of violence (Cortés had defeated the Tabascan chief who then gave Malinche to him as a "present"). It follows that Malinche-doña Marina marks the hegemony that replaces brute force, a hegemony based on a contract that functions as a result of previous violence. Hegemony has to operate *as if* subjects were to freely choose their subaltern position. Malinche does not represent Indians in the sense of *vertreten*, but of *Darstellung*, that is, in the sense of representation as that which instantiates hegemony. (Franco, 2001)

We can trace both the mestizo nationalist origin myth and the myth of Isthmus Zapotec matriarchy to the nationalist cultural imagination cultivated within the post-revolutionary state. On one hand, we have a nationalist discourse that constructs gender, ethnic, and national identities along a rigid binary opposition between dominator and dominated, masculine hispanicity and feminine indigeneity; on the other, we have a revolutionary discourse that looks to a remote horizon onto which it can project its utopian longing for a location where past, present, and future escape the dynamics of colonial subjugation.

Positing an alter-ego relationship between these two myths allows us a first glimpse into the internal ideological struggle within revolutionary nationalism: namely, whether to acknowledge that Mexico is a multiethnic society struggling collectively to overcome Spanish and then Creole minority rule, the path alluded to by Ricardo Flores Magón ([1914] 1997), or to assimilate its heterogeneous elements into a Spanish-speaking mestizo ideal, as Gamio ([1916] 1960) would have it. Between the myth of Malinche and the myth of matriarchal utopia there are some fundamental differences: first, as a historical figure Malinche is central to the mythology of modern Mexican national identity. The Tehuana maiden of Rivera's and others' reveries, on the other hand, is envisioned as an ideal type, a utopian figure echoing the promise of what Mexico would be like if "she" had not been conquered and perhaps, what she might be like if and when the promise of Revolution is fulfilled. The myth of Isthmus Zapotec matriarchy, as it has been elaborated in the visual and literary works we have discussed here, represents the wild, unconscious or pre-modern element that has yet to be domesticated, Paz's "underground stream" or Gamio's "blood and soil." The strong and elegant Istmeña is thus a symbol for that which is exterior to Mexican national identity but which the post-revolutionary state attempts to capture and "wear" as a trophy; in contrast, Malinche symbolizes the central yet disembodied interior core of Mexican national identity, the Indian, feminine, shameful element that should be hidden from view.

This problem is significant because the ideology of mestizo nationalism, which demands that indigenous ancestry be hidden and dissolved, has left no space within which diverse groups of indigenous people might advance their own understandings of gender, sexual, ethnic, and national identities. Instead, it has cast "the Indian" as a mute collective singular entity whose "incoherent" local economic, cultural, and political forms of organization present obstacles to modernization and progress. Forged in the revolutionary struggle as a means of unifying an ethno-linguistically diverse group of peasants and workers against the landed oligarchy, mestizo nationalism was then rearticulated by post-revolutionary elites in their bid to construct a centralized state with which this diverse group might come to identify. Within this configuration, Isthmus Zapotec culture then becomes that indissoluble element, that other against which Mexican national identity may be defined.

Today, as global markets eclipse national governments as producers of "cultural metaphors of citizenship" (Saldaña-Portillo, 2003, 210), the types of mestizo nationalist or indigenista cultural production are being replaced by a government discourse of multiculturalism and the promotion of ethno-linguistic diversity. The cancellation of indigenista-planned acculturation policies and the creation of government-sponsored circuits of indigenous cultural production must be understood in part as a response to indigenous movements for cultural autonomy, particularly since the 1994 Zapatista revolt. The state's official multiculturalist pronouncements must be analyzed as a cultural corollary to its neoliberal economic policies such as the North American Free Trade Agreement and the proposed Plan Puebla-Panamá that threaten the livelihood of indigenous peasants, and indigenous women in particular. Mestizo nationalist discourses of normative citizenship and indigenista policies of ethno-linguistic assimilation have lent a benevolent veneer to the nationally oriented agro-industrial development projects of the twentieth century. These projects have subverted indigenous peasants' attempts to implement land reform and have worked to forcibly incorporate indigenous communities into relations of increasing dependence on wage labor and export-oriented agriculture. As Saldaña-Portillo argues, the Zapatistas "were not somehow left out of Mexico's discourse of development" but instead "have emerged from within revolutionary policies of agrarian reform and agricultural development" (2003, 213). As Comandante Esther affirms in her address to the National Congress, it is imperative for indigenous women to have access to political channels that would allow them to represent themselves and to challenge the role that mestizo nationalism has reserved for them in national state formation, a role that dictates that women—and especially indigenous women—exist only insofar as they exist for others.

We can appreciate the contrast between this formulation and the portrait Gosling (*Blossoms of Fire*, 2000) paints of Juchitec women's and muxes' relationships to the public sphere, where feminine identity is synonymous with the capacity to earn a livelihood and to determine the conditions of personal and collective dignity. But here I must insist that many of the purportedly matriarchal elements found in Isthmus Zapotec culture can also be found throughout Mexican society. If we look, we can see that women all over Mexico serve as administrators of family finances and informal networks of community organization. Much of what we point to as evidence of matriarchy among Isthmus Zapotecs can be found in other parts of Mexico, but we have been conditioned to turn a blind eye to it, to notice only the machismo that Paz considered synonymous with mexicanidad.

By presenting a politically, sexually, and economically liberating portrait of a specific ethnic group within Mexico, representations of Isthmus Zapotecs as exceptionally gynocentric run the risk of tacitly feeding into mainstream representations of Mexican society as inherently *machista*. In the service of the post-revolutionary single party state, both the myth of Isthmus Zapotec matriarchy and the myth of abject indigenous femininity embodied in the figure of Malinche have enabled the perpetuation of mestizo nationalist hegemony.

At the same time, as they are both ultimately cultural metaphors of the Indian woman as *non-citizen*, as constitutive of yet outside national identity, they have also contained within them the terms most useful for dismantling the national popular state's patriarchal and racist models of citizenship. Nationalist discourses that construct gender, ethnic, and national identities along a rigid binary opposition between dominator and dominated, masculine hispanicity and feminine indigeneity have become anachronistic at the present moment of globalization. The feminization of labor that has characterized the transition from an import substitution model of economic development to the export-oriented, socially austere model also transforms the *face* of labor, such that, as Serret affirms: "we are witnessing a pulverization of identity referents that, it would seem, will inevitably give way to the existence of multiple feminine identities in a collective sense" (1999, 273). What would Mexican national identity look like if the myth of Malinche no longer dominated primary school history textbooks and political discourse? Perhaps the libidinal energies trapped within the myth of Malinche and the counter-myth of Isthmus Zapotec exceptionality could then be channeled into the recognition of Mexico's pluricultural and sexually multivalent reality. Turning around these myths, as Comandante Esther asserts, can only begin with the constitutional recognition of the rights of diverse groups to pursue cultural, economic, and political horizons that depart from those favored by the federal government and international capitalist interests.[6]

Conclusion

On August 2, 2000, Mexico City's National Museum of Anthropology hosted the unveiling of "Cultural Diversity in Mexico: Indigenous Communities and their Sixty-two Languages." Resembling middle-school maps that indicate where to find key natural resources, the diversity map features brightly illustrated, neatly labeled Indians living in harmony with the natural world from sparse northwestern desert to dense southeastern jungle. It presents the viewer with a portrait of an idyllic Mexico, unmarred by *maquiladoras*, military bases, or urbanization. Under the auspices of the Public Ministry of Education (Secretaría de Educación Pública, SEP), and the National Council of Culture and Arts (Consejo Nacional Para la Cultura y las Artes, CONACULTA), poster-sized reproductions of the map were distributed to a limited number of public schools, cultural centers, and museums.

The diversity map is intended to promote respect for indigenous communities, languages, and regions. In this sense, it contrasts with the predominant image of "the Indian"—homogenous, childlike, and not yet fully Mexican—found in mid-century ethnographies and elementary school textbooks.[1] The map represents an institutional move away from official indigenismo as assimilationist cultural politics and toward a new official affirmation of cultural pluralism.

What does the inauguration of this diversity map indicate about the changing face of indigeneity in Mexican national culture at the beginning of the twentieth century? This map sums up the central question examined throughout this book: who represents indigenous peoples—in both an aesthetic-cultural and a political-legal sense—and toward what ends? Instead of simply congratulating the government for recognizing and even celebrating ethnic and cultural pluralism, I would like to suggest here that

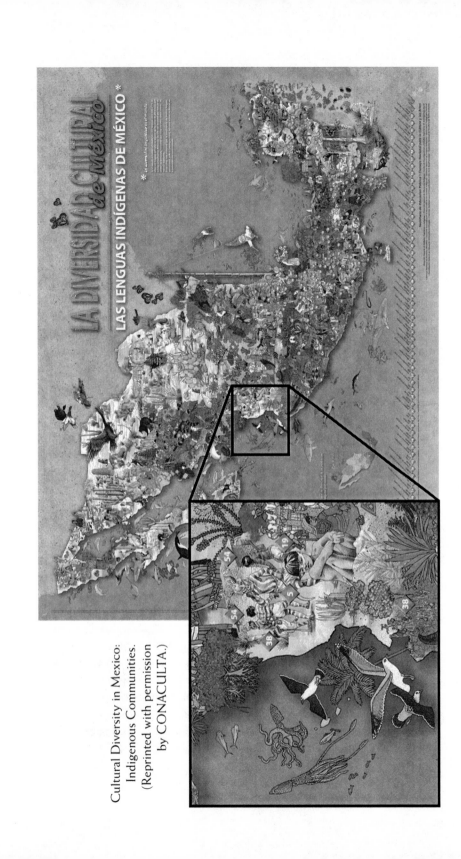

LA DIVERSIDAD CULTURAL
de méxico

LAS LENGUAS INDÍGENAS DE MÉXICO*

Cultural Diversity in Mexico:
Indigenous Communities.
(Reprinted with permission
by CONACULTA.)

the map actually represents an instance in which the government recycles its old concepts of indigenous culture in order to manage the claims indigenous groups have been posing about their rights as citizens of Mexico and as first peoples in the Americas. The diversity map reflects how state social and cultural agencies have updated the storehouse of ideas and images of indigenous peoples and national belonging that they have inherited from their revolutionary nationalist past. Since the 1980s and particularly in the past ten years of Zapatista struggle, these institutions have begun to make cultural diversity, rather than cultural assimilation, their central concern.

State agencies are reformulating their approach to indigenous peoples in two related ways: first, with the dismantling of the social welfare model since the early 1980s, the state directs much less funding and support for the institutions that have created indigenista policies and cultural production; second, with the limited infrastructure it has maintained for these institutions, the state focuses its efforts on mimicking the different ideas, images, and vocabularies used by indigenous groups and social movements in order to divert the challenges these movements pose to the hegemony of ruling elites.

The inauguration of this diversity map on the grounds of the National Museum of Anthropology heralds a profound transformation in how these agencies and the intellectuals associated with them represent indigenous cultural identity. The National Museum of Anthropology has played a central role as the symbolic location for the dramatization of a national popular discourse of race in Mexico. As Ernesto Garcia Canclini has argued, since its opening by President Adolfo López Mateos in 1964, the high modernist building's grand-scale displays have consistently stressed the grandeur of the pre-conquest (particularly Aztec) past on the ground floor while promoting a stagnant, superficial profile of present-day indigenous communities on the top floor. This architectural split has established a cognitive framework in which the nation's treasured cultural patrimony (the Mesoamerican past) does not belong to the indigenous peoples of today.[2] The content and spatial organization of the second floor reinforces the indigenista notion that living indigenous communities are stuck in a cycle of reproducing a fixed set of cultural practices, instead of actively producing culture.

In contrast, this map announces the failure of the indigenista paradigm; it calls attention to the fact that the Mexican population is *not* becoming more ethnically, linguistically, or culturally homogenized, despite nearly six decades of state-sponsored programs designed to assimilate indigenous groups to an abstract mestizo ideal. Officiating the inauguration of the diversity map were three Mexican writers, two of them non-indigenous and widely recognized as scholars and promoters of indigenous literatures and human rights: Miguel León Portilla and Carlos Montemayor. The third distinguished presenter, Natalio Hernández is celebrated as one of Mexico's most important living writers of indigenous language poetry, fiction, and essays. Unlike the first two, his photograph did not appear in the newspapers the following day; yet his key role in this inaugural event represents perhaps the most dramatic shift in the way indigenous peoples are represented within state-run cultural institutions in Mexico. As a Nahuatl poet, professor, and cultural critic who writes and publishes in both Spanish and Nahuatl, Hernández's participation in this event as an *agent*—a protagonist in this apparent renegotiation of the dominant discourse of race—calls into question the content of the rest of the museum, which represents living indigenous peoples as mute and quaintly frozen in time at the periphery of the nation's modernity. Will more indigenous writers such as Natalio Hernández begin to reshape the field of cultural production in Mexico? Or will it continue to be rare that indigenous Mexicans find a space in which to represent themselves and their communities in national and international spheres and earn a living from their intellectual work? As Hernández's central role in this event suggests, it is no longer a given that political and cultural representations of indigenous peoples will be produced exclusively by non-indigenous hands and minds.

The dismantling of the welfare state model has had, and will continue to have, far-reaching effects on the ways in which contemporary indigenous peoples, as well as their pre-Hispanic heritage, are represented. In order to understand what is at stake in this institutional move toward what Consuelo Sánchez calls "participatory indigenismo,"[3] it is imperative to take a closer look at the tension between this institutional reformulation of indigeneity on one hand and how indigenous people challenge dominant formulations of indigeneity in neoliberal times. Indigenous and peasant groups have gained visibility and international solidarity as they demand human rights and control over their lands and resources. State cultural institutions have reoriented themselves toward a new project of lending the neoliberal state an aura of multicultural tolerance, even as that state expands its military presence around indigenous communities.

As Gareth Williams observes in *The Other Side of the Popular*, the narratives and symbols of social identity consecrated by the national popular state have come to appear as ideological and aesthetic fossils in the last quarter century in Latin America. He notes that throughout much of the twentieth century the national popular state had stimulated and disseminated narratives of a unified and ethnically homogenous *pueblo* under its authoritarian cloak. Yet since the early 1980s, a wave of debt crises and subsequent socioeconomic austerity policies have led the state to withdraw from its previous role as social benefactor and guardian of national cultural patrimony. The neoliberal heir to the national popular state is thus haunted by the institutional remnants and symbols of cultural nationalism.

As Williams asserts, the ascendance of transnational capitalism over national economies radically alters the grounds on which cultural production and the construction of social identities take shape in Latin America.[4] Just as the concept of "national economy" sounds anachronistic to us today, the concept of "national culture," which had become so central to our understandings of Latin American literary and artistic expression, has entered an equally nebulous phase. Claudio Lomnitz's observations in *Deep Mexico, Silent Mexico* (2001) regarding the role of the social sciences and particularly anthropology in this post-national moment put this transformation in vivid terms:

> The crisis in anthropology today is not as much about the discipline's absorption by the state as it is about its uncertain role in the marketplace. An enlightened vanguard may no longer realistically aspire to fashion and shape public opinion for internal purposes, and discourses regarding cultural origins and social hierarchies are no longer central to the allure of the country for foreign governments and capitalists. In this sense, there is a real need for invention. (233)

Lomnitz notes that the post-revolutionary state's capacity to construct a "convincing national teleology" (233) capable of drawing a diverse group of peasants and workers into its corporatist state structure has been trumped by the exigencies of the transnational corporation, which, like the state, is a pseudo-personage, but unlike the state, has no apparent use for "discourses regarding cultural origins and social hierarchies" (233). Hence there is little need to generate or control cultural production or specialized knowledge about different sectors of society. The tenuous ground on which intellectual production finds itself within this new configuration of market, state, and society is a consequence of the increasing privatization of cultural circuits (and pauperization of their state-run counterparts) that has gone hand-in-hand with the privatization of large sectors of the Mexican economy in the past quarter century. This leads us to ask what kinds of narratives of cultural identity, if any, are promoted both from within the post-national remnants of state social and cultural institutions as well as from within the market-driven privatized educational, publishing, and artistic circuits. The map of ethno-linguistic diversity and the circumstances of its inauguration are symptomatic of how indigenismo has been superseded on some levels yet continues to reinscribe on others. This reinscription of the Indian as other is due to the fact that non-indigenous peoples and institutions run by non-indigenous peoples still ultimately organize intellectual and cultural circuits, particularly in Mexico City. Indigenous peoples' full participation in these circuits is growing yet still remains marginal and dependent on urban mestizo intellectuals to act as mediators and promoters.

In this context, we can look at the diversity map as a reenactment of the dynamic we have seen throughout this book. Indigenismo acts as a hegemonic discourse of national belonging and social marginality; yet in its representations of marginality, it constitutes one of the few spaces where a critique of state discourses and policies can emerge. Today, it remains to be seen whether the field of cultural production in Mexico will continue to be a site from which terms of social inclusion and exclusion are delineated, or if instead, cultural production will become a site through which these terms are finally cancelled out by those who have been barred from participating in the circuits of national intellectual life.

Changes in the way indigeneity has been constructed in the Mexican cultural imagination have occurred in the context of two interrelated factors: on one hand, the escalating debt crises and subsequent liberalization of the Mexican economy in the past few decades have hastened the demise of the welfare state model. The complex network of state agencies that have been built up around the PRI have found themselves underfinanced and with an unclear role in a state which has now relinquished its former narratives of national origin and destiny.[5] On the other hand, autonomous indigenous movements that have emerged in this recent period have called attention to the state's failure to address indigenous peoples on their own terms. The diversity map shows us how indigenismo is being reformulated from within these institutions in order to meet the state's new political goals at a moment of transition as the PRI finds itself edged out of political dominance by the conservative National Action Party (PAN).

Given the unprecedented budget cuts and tuition hikes at public universities, as well as the rapid growth of privatized education and cultural institutions such as museums and publishing houses, it was hardly a surprise when in May of 2003 President Vicente Fox announced his decision to close the ailing INI and open a smaller agency, the Consejo Nacional para el Desarollo de los Pueblos Indígenas (National Council for the Development of Indigenous Communities or CONADEPI). Critics argue that the CONADEPI adopts the rhetoric of indigenous self-determination but lacks clear institutional mechanisms through which it might mediate between indigenous peoples and the state. This reorganization of indigenista imperatives and policies comes at a crucial moment in which questions of indigenous autonomy and cultural survival have yet to be addressed by the federal government. The CONADEPI and other institutions ignore the fact that indigenous peoples are supporting organizations like Sección 22 of the Oaxacan teachers' association. Within this context, we can see that the CONADEPI fails to participate in the resolution of conflicts between the government and indigenous/mestizo peoples' struggles for human rights.

As Margarita Nolasco notes, the CONADEPI lacks concrete proposals either to integrate or to grant autonomy to indigenous peoples in Mexico.[6] Clearly, it would be absurd to mourn the passing of a government agency that has epitomized the paternalism and authoritarianism of the Mexican ruling party state. At the same time, we can hardly celebrate the attenuation of state-sponsored indigenismo; it does not appear that it is being replaced with a genuine platform from which indigenous peoples might have some latitude in defining for themselves an acceptable relationship to the state.

Indigenismo Unraveled

As we have seen throughout this book, the question of who represents indigenous peoples, in a political as well as an aesthetic or symbolic sense, and for what purposes, have been the subjects of intense debate among intellectuals and indigenous leaders, particularly since the late 1960s and early 1970s.[7] Critiques of political and cultural representation of indigenous peoples have largely centered upon the role of the INI. These critics have argued that since its creation in the 1940s, the agency has promoted a paternalistic vision of "our Indians" as remote in time and space, a homogeneous collective entity to be acted upon or influenced, defiled or improved, but whose members could not conceivably participate in defining what it means to be indigenous in Mexico.

Yet in the early 1980s, under the presidency of Miguel de la Madrid, it became evident that the Mexican ruling party was rapidly trading its national popular agenda of import substitution and nationalized industry for a model of state development based on catering to transnational investors and the trimming of the social welfare function of the state. However, wholesale privatization and cuts in social programs did not square with the revolutionary nationalist image upon which the PRI had constructed its hegemony. At this point, the PRI began to tone down that image, avoiding the once common references to the Revolution, letting go of anti-imperialist rhetoric, no longer addressing the public as *pueblo mexicano* but instead, as *compatriotas* (compatriots) and later, after the Zapatista uprising, mirroring subcomandante Marcos's inclusive *mexicanas y mexicanos*. The debt crisis, combined with the internal conflicts brewing within the INI, has left the indigenista project of appropriation and assimilation of indigenous culture into national culture with severely weakened institutional mechanisms and with an even-less-clear purpose. At the same time, appropriation still occurs on a grand scale; this time indigenous cultures are commodified in the international marketplace.

The image of indigeneity has also been internationalized as an important element in indigenous struggles for self-determination and human rights. The classic indigenista portrait of the isolated indigenous community as a quaint anachronism en route to extinction or assimilation on which indigenista action was based has proven to be a chimera of functionalist anthropology. In academic terms, this folkloric image has become increasingly obsolete today, as indigenous peasants faced with agricultural crisis migrate farther and more permanently from their communities.[8] However, this image continues to hold an allure for consumers and tourists.

While indigenismo played a fundamental role in bolstering the PRI's state-as-benefactor image, it has proven to be an especially ineffective mechanism for dealing with the globally connected indigenous and popular movements that have gained visibility in recent years. The Zapatista uprising of 1994 created a radical break with the ways in which indigenous peoples had been represented, in a political as well as a cultural sense. Putting global telecommunications to work for them against economic globalization, this uprising has called the country's (and the world's) attention to the persistence of a caste-like social structure. Indigenous activists, writers, and artists (and many of their non-indigenous allies) question the underlying social conditions that have permitted the most widely circulating images, discourses, and policies regarding ethnically indigenous peoples to have been created almost exclusively from non-indigenous perspectives. The institutional move away from indigenismo and toward multiculturalism, exemplified by the diversity map, can thus be understood as a strategy to manage and redirect the radical propositions of these movements in ways that do not alter the basic power relations between rulers and ruled, a "neohegemonic stabilization of the subaltern's destabilizing force,"[9] as Gareth Williams might have it. It is in this sense that the denouement of official indigenismo looks a lot like its beginning in 1940s Mexico.

Indigeneity and the Marketplace of Images

Perceptions and projections of indigenous peoples and indigenous *being*, of the place and power of indigenous ethnic groups, languages, and forms of social organization within Mexican society have undergone radical changes in recent decades. Take a stroll through any tourist market or plaza in Mexico City eyeing the ubiquitous reproductions of Diego Rivera's smoothly rounded earthen figures stooping under the weight of gigantic calla lilies; turn on the television to the buffoonish caricatures of *el indito* in reruns of popular films from the Golden Age of Mexican cinema. Better yet, visit the National Museum of Anthropology to peruse the stone splendors of pre-conquest Mesoamerica; but before museum exhaustion sets in, go upstairs to ponder the 1960s dioramas of faceless rag dolls condemned to an endless, frozen engagement with their daily labors and festivities. These institutionalized stereotypes of an eloquently silent or abject Indian persist in Mexico's cultural imaginary, but they linger as fossilized relics of a bygone era, one in which images of indigeneity had been molded exclusively by non-Indian hands and minds.

Such romanticized or denigrated emblems of indigeneity now compete with indigenous photographic, filmic, and literary works, poster-sized reproductions of the Taniperlas mural memorializing the 1997 massacre of Acteal, and countless photos, dolls, T-shirts, books, and CDs featuring masked EZLN comandantes. In Mexico City bookstores, faded and yellowed mid-century indigenista novels and ethnographies lose shelf space to newly printed bilingual editions of indigenous short stories, poetry, and photo-essays. These exuberant displays of indigenous art, photography, and literature surely herald a sea change in the contours of Mexican cultural production that is only beginning to make waves. Today, organized indigenous groups stand out in their refusal to allow their cultures to be reduced to museum displays and their languages to linguistics textbooks, particularly when they are precluded from having a hand in shaping the images and discourses that depict them.[10]

This juxtaposition of conflicting images and ideas about what it means to be Indian in Mexico does not merely reflect a change in aesthetic prerogatives; it is indicative of profound transformations in the social, economic, and political conditions in which these types of representations are produced. Such divergent emblems of indigeneity in the crowded marketplace of cultural products do not just vie for tourist dollars; they also compete for validation of radically opposed social projects. These conflicting images are symptomatic of a bitterly stalemated debate regarding the terms of inclusion of indigenous peoples in Mexican national political life and international law.

In the fourteen years since the initial 1994 EZLN uprising, the abyss between indigenous leaders' ideas of what it will take to ensure indigenous rights and cultural survival and government officials' responses to those claims appears to have widened precipitously. Official dialogues between the Maya comandantes of the EZLN and Mexican Congressional negotiators resulted in the forging of the San Andrés Accords, signed by both parties on February 16, 1996, under the administration of President Ernesto Zedillo. This document mandated changes to the Mexican constitution that would ensure a significant measure of legal, political, economic, and cultural autonomy to indigenous groups to facilitate Mexico's compliance with United Nations Resolution 169, which the federal government had previously ratified in September 1990.[11] Yet the San Andrés Accords have been summarily reinterpreted and ignored, first by the Zedillo administration and more recently by that of President Vicente Fox and his successor, Felipe Calderón. The central unresolved question that has kept these accords on a bureaucratic shelf has been whether autonomy guarantees land and subsoil rights, as the Zapatistas would have it, or merely the right to cultural self-expression in an abstract sense without significant changes to the Mexican constitution, as the federal government would have it (Weinberg, 2000, 8).

In the twelve years since the signing of the Peace Accords, the Mexican government has pursued a convoluted strategy of conciliation and repression when dealing with indigenous demands for economic, political, and cultural autonomy. In its public, conciliatory mood, the governing elite has incorporated the multiculturalist and anti-sexist language of Zapatismo into its own political rhetoric and sponsored initiatives aimed to foment indigenous cultural expression. Yet in its covert, repressive mood, it has escalated military and paramilitary operations within indigenous communities struggling to exercise their autonomy in political and economic terms.

For indigenous leaders, the concept of regional autonomy continues to center upon control over ancestral lands and the resources contained or potentially contained within them. Indigenous cultural survival, as articulated by indigenous leaders throughout the Americas and the world, stems from the right to strive for a harmonious relationship between agriculture and culture, even when that relationship foreshortens the potential for capital accumulation in and around those ancestral lands. Yet for the Mexican government, regional autonomy has meant *anything but* that primary right to exercise control over land and resources.

This dispute over the meaning of indigenous cultural survival and the means through which it can be fostered brings to the foreground the question of how the term culture—and namely indigenous culture—continues to be defined in radically opposite terms within the workings of grassroots movements for indigenous autonomy on one hand and within state cultural and social agencies on the other.

Indigeneity: Between Race, Class, and Culture

The inauguration of the Instituto Nacional Indigenista (INI) in the late 1940s was a watershed and an impasse, a critical moment in which the categories *peasant* and *Indian* were discursively de-linked. The "Indian problem" replaced the agrarian problem in official discourse, such that at issue was now social behavior rather than social structure. It was politically safer to discuss indigenous culture and language rather than indigenous rights to land, water, and local political control. At present, the possibility of relinking these identities, of facing the agrarian crisis through the affirmation of cultural and ethno-linguistic heterogeneity, and through the affirmation of indigenous knowledge as knowledge, rather than simply as cultural idiosyncrasy, might offer the conditions from which to rise above the indigenista impasse and make way for more coherent and empowering forms of political and cultural representation.

Yet the contradictions to be found in participatory or multicultural indigenismo stem from the fact that indigenous peoples do not have a clean slate upon which to represent themselves, but instead must reckon with the ways in which they have been barred from self-representation and self-determination within the national sphere. The ideal conditions for autonomous indigenous cultural production would render superfluous the mediation of non-indigenous agents who ultimately determine its form and control its use, distribution, and revenue. The current attenuation of the post-revolutionary cultural institutions that were put in place to assure the unification and homogenization of national identity does not lead unequivocally to the possibility for autonomous indigenous cultural and political representation. Paradoxically, the much-talked-about nationalization of indigenous struggles is taking place at a moment of radical de-nationalization of the Mexican economy. The question of who represents indigenous people, and to what ends, is perhaps less clear today than it was before the 1980s.

Indigenous and popular social movements seek to determine for themselves who will be their protagonists and how they will lead within their struggles. However, several things have inhibited this process. Until very recently, the Mexican state has been reasonably successful in curtailing the formation of indigenous organic intellectuals by making non-indigenous interlocutors or mediators central to the relationship between indigenous groups and the state. Thus, one of the Zapatista National Liberation Army's cornerstone demands has been that the government fund and implement bilingual and culturally sensitive public education in order to give indigenous people the opportunity to articulate the needs and aspirations of their communities and contribute on their own terms to the country's development. Yet today, government policies remain centered on bringing development to indigenous communities, rather than recognizing any degree of sovereignty or autonomy within them.

We have seen that official indigenismo's foundational moment intersected with the post-revolutionary governing elite's bid for agro-industrial modernization and concentration of political power. To maintain its power, this elite both used and eschewed the popular mandate for land reform that had fueled the Revolution of 1910. Today, the unraveling of the INI and subsequent opening of the much-less ambitious CONADEPI provides us with the opportunity to come face to face with the social conflicts that both of these government offices have been created to repress. The persistent feature of these clumsy institutional attempts to represent indigeneity is that they continue to define indigenous culture in truncated terms: culture truncated from its own ancestry (as the nod of approval for the construction of the Wal-Mart near Teotihuacan demonstrates), and culture truncated from land and livelihood (as the failure to modify the Mexican Constitution to honor the San Andrés Accords clearly demonstrates). The impasse between the post-revolutionary government's formulation of "the Indian problem" and the aspirations of indigenous and mestizo peasants for "land and liberty" has never been resolved within state-sponsored indigenismo.

The cancellation of the INI in 2003 represents the shedding of one of the last vestiges of the national-popular state. Yet as long as it continues to define indigenous culture in terms of *usos y costumbres*, as customs and traditions, the CONADEPI or any other state agency will be incapable of solving the "Indian problem," which the state has created by its own hand. As it turns out, the "Indian problem" is not really Indian at all, but is instead a government problem wearing a stolen Indian mask.

Notes

Introduction

1. This and subsequent translations are mine unless otherwise noted. For the full text of Subcomandante Esther's Speech, see http://geocities.com/tierray libertad _ac/indigenas/cdtaesther.htm. Accessed Oct. 23, 2008.

2. For an analysis of indigenismo prior to the 1940s, see Alexander S. Dawson, *Indian and Nation in Revolutionary Mexico* (Tucson: University of Arizona Press, 2004).

Chapter 1. Applied Anthropology and Post-revolutionary State Consolidation

1. To replace the 55-year-old agency, President Fox created the National Commission for the Development of Indigenous Communities (CONADEPI). Critics have noted that the CONADEPI has been concocted with the same paternalistic and bureaucratic recipes of the ailing INI at its most anemic phase, sidestepping vital questions of regional self-government, control over natural resources, and human rights. See Magdalena Gómez, "Indigenismo del cambio?" *La Jornada* (May 2003); and Carlos Montemayor, "Adiós al INI," *La Jornada* (May 2003).

2. As Judith Friedlander observes, "More often than not, what is identified as Indian is actually of Spanish colonial origin." *Being Indian in Hueyapan: A Study of Forced Identity in Contemporary Mexico* (New York: St. Martin's Press, 1975), 100. For example, native dress is often used as an indicator of authenticity, yet much of those dress styles date back to the colonial period, when they were imposed on native groups in order to facilitate their distinction and control their movement between villages and colonial settlements. Additionally, she argues that forms of collective association generally considered native, such as municipalities and cargo systems, are often adaptations of colonially imposed religious, economic, and political organization.

3. The list of Mexican delegates includes Manuel Gamio, Alfonso Caso, Miguel O. de Mendizábal, and Moisés Sáenz, all of whom played key roles in

the development of applied anthropology and the institutionalization of the INI. Two of the earliest indigenista fiction writers, Mauricio Magdaleno and Ermilo Abreu Gómez, were also present. See chapters three and four for an analysis of the relationship between official indigenismo and indigenista literary production from the 1930s to the 1960s. At the First Inter-American Indigenist Conference, the social discourse of race was being defined within the context of industrialization and the acceleration of political and economic links between the rural and urban populations. At the same time, the United States government was beginning to pursue its "good neighbor" policy. Influencing and keeping close tabs on the development of social discourse and social policy in Latin America was an important element in this overall program to gain control of Latin American markets. Oscar L. Chapman, *Final Proceedings of the First Inter-American Conference on Indian Life* (Washington D.C.: U.S. Office of Indian Affairs, 1940), 7–8. [Transl. of *Acta final del primer Congreso indigenista interamericano* (Washington D.C.: Unión Panamericana, 1940), serie sobre Congresos y Conferencias, n. 30].

4. Ibid., 46.

5. Ibid., 11.

6. Stephen R. Niblo, *Mexico in the 1940s* (Wilmington, DE: Scholarly Resources, 1999), 333–35. See also Dan Hofstader, *Mexico: 1946–73* (New York: Facts on File, 1974), 36–38.

7. Chapman, 7–8.

8. Ibid.

9. "*Ejidatarios* have non-transferable usufruct rights to individual plots, unless they decide collective use is preferable. Communal ownership and administration existed 'in perpetuity' until the guarantee was abolished under President Salinas' neoliberal regime in 1991." See subcomandante Marcos and the Zapatista Army of National Liberation, *Shadows of Tender Fury*, transl. Frank Bardacke, Leslie Lopez, and the Watsonville, California Staff Human Rights Committee (New York: Monthly Review Press, 1995), 269.

10. See also Roger Bartra's discussion of the relationship between Cárdenas's populism and a later populist *caudillismo* or bossism. According to Bartra, "The Mexican Revolution is the history of the struggles and alliances between the bourgeoisie and the peasantry, a history that transpires in the midst of unsettling contradictions between the interests of a politically impotent peasantry and a sector of the bourgeoisie that cannot find a clear political alternative to the patterns of the porfirian landholding bourgeoisie that had just been defeated. The class alliance and the reformist pact Lázaro Cárdenas achieved 20 years after the 'official' end of the Revolution constituted a political solution to these contradictions and the point of departure for the current Mexican system. . . . [However,] the class alliance established by Cárdenas, in which some form of mediated peasant participation in the political sphere is virtually broken between 1940 and 1946." Roger Bartra, *Caciquismo y poder político en el México rural* (Mexico: Siglo XXI Editores, 1975), 25.

11. As Juan Rulfo depicts in the short story "Nos han dado la tierra," much of the land granted to peasants by the post-revolutionary government was unsuitable for cultivation. In that story, the single drop of rain that evaporates upon contact with the parched desert earth symbolizes the empty gestures the new government performs in place of the deep reforms necessary to redistribute property and privilege. When the story's protagonists attempt to appeal to the government for better land, they are faced with a cruel bureaucratic runaround that leaves them empty-handed since their illiteracy excludes them from engaging in an appeals process. Juan Rulfo, "Nos han dado la tierra," in *El llano en llamas* (Mexico: Fondo de Cultura Económica, 1998), 9–15.

12. Gonzalo Aguirre Beltrán, *Teoría y práctica de la educación indígena* (Mexico: Fondo de Cultura Económica, 1992), 134.

13. Consuelo Ros Romero, *La imágen del indio en el discurso del Instituto Nacional Indigenista* (Mexico: CIESAS, 1992), 11–12. See also pp. 96, 106, 116–19.

14. Arturo Warman et al., *De eso que llaman antropología mexicana* (Mexico City: Nuestro Tiempo, 1971); and Andrés Medina and Carlos García Mora, *La quiebra política de la antropología social en México* (Mexico: UNAM, 1986).

15. Rodolfo Stavenhagen, *Sociología y subdesarrollo* (Mexico City: Nuestro Tiempo, 1971); and Pablo González Casanova, *La democracia en México* (Mexico City: Ediciones Era, 1965).

Chapter 2. Narrating the Indian as Other: Foundational Indigenista Fictions

1. Severing the link between the pre-conquest indigenous past and the post-colonial indigenous and mestizo present, *indigenismo* constructs the native past as the center of national identity, locating it in the nation's capital, the cradle of *Mexica* civilization. Thus, all *capitalinos* (inhabitants of Mexico City), no matter what their genetic makeup, can draw national pride from this glorious past. Living indigenous groups play an equally important role in the definition of national identity; while the indigenous past constitutes the core of Mexican identity, the indigenous present constitutes its periphery, the *other* against which the national, modern, urban subject may define himself. I say "*himself*" because the national subject, along with the indigenous past is gendered male, as the indigenous present is infantilized and gendered female. See Natividad Gutiérrez, *Nationalist Myths and Ethnic Identities: Indigenous Intellectuals and the Mexican State* (Lincoln: University of Nebraska Press, 1999).

2. For Serge Gruzinski, simulacrum "inclusively designates, in classical Latin, a figurative meaning, an effigy, a material representation of ideas, a shadow, and a ghost." *Images at War*, trans. Heather MacLean (Durham, NC: Duke University Press, 2001), 231.

3. Doris Sommer defines *costumbrismo* in terms that liken it to a particularly self-congratulatory and insipid shade of transculturation: "Perhaps as much in Spanish America as in the Spain that Larra spoke for, the function of costumbrismo was 'to make the different strata of society comprehensible to one

another.'" *Foundational Fictions: The National Romances of Latin America* (Berkeley: University of California Press, 1991), 14. As I see it, *Tremendismo* (or *miserabilismo*), a literary style best exemplified by that infamous allegory of the Spanish Civil War, *La familia de Pascual Duarte*, would simply be the hard-core flip side of costumbrismo, whereby the vision of a quaintly heterogeneous and idiosyncratic society gives way to an open intolerance and hostility toward those radically heterogeneous elements.

4. Donald L. Schmidt, "Changing Narrative Techniques in the Mexican Indigenista Novel," Ph.D diss. University of Kansas, 1972: 38.

5. Rosario Castellanos's feminist treatment of *indigenista* themes in *Balún Canán* (Fondo de Cultura Económica: México, 1959) and *Oficio de tinieblas* (México: Juaquín Mortiz, 1962) revisits and perhaps subverts this white male gaze upon the productive countryside and the related reduction of indigenous female characters to reproductive vessels. See chapter three.

Chapter 3. *The Ethnographic Coming-of-age Story*

1. Thomas E. Skidmore and Peter H. Smith, *Modern Latin America* (New York: Oxford University Press, 2001), 233–24; and T. R. Fehrenbach, *Fire and Blood* (New York: Da Capo Press, 1995), 602–28. For an excellent analysis of rural to urban migration, see *Americas: Continent on the Move*, part 3, dir. Raymond Telles and Marc de Beaufort (WGBH Educational Foundation, 1993).

2. Telles, Raymond, and Marc de Beaufort, dirs. *Americas: Continent on the Move*. part 3. (WGBH Educational Foundation, 1993).

3. Gonzalo Aguirre Beltrán, *Teoría y práctica de la educación indígena* (Mexico: Fondo de Cultura Económica, 1992), 132–45.

4. Ricardo Pozas, *Chamula* (Mexico City: Instituto Nacional Indigenista, 1979) 1: 216.

5. Antonio Rodríguez Chicharro, *La novela indigenista mexicana* (Mexico City: UNAM, 1962), 116.

6. Carlos Lenkersdorf, *Los hombres verdaderos: voces y testimonios tojolabales* (Mexico City: Siglo XXI, 1996).

7. This opening of the novel demonstrates Castellanos's familiarity with Tzotzil oral tradition. Enrique Pérez López, "Religion Amongst Indigenous People of Today," *Indigenous Voices* 5 (January/February 1998):34–35.

8. For an excellent exposition on language in the work of Castellanos, see René Prieto, *Body of Writing: Figuring Desire in Spanish American Literature* (Durham, NC: Duke University Press, 2000), 172–212.

9. Like sinister gatekeepers, throughout the novel *mestizos* are characterized as inhabiting the threshold between two radically distinct worlds, doing the dirty work of victimizing indigenous people for the benefit of the *coletos*; they are always cast as *enganchadores*, *atajadoras*, prostitutes, and petty authorities.

10. Doris Sommer, introduction of *Proceed with Caution, when Engaged by Minority Writing in the Americas* (Cambridge, MA: Harvard University Press, 1999).

11. Joseph Sommers, "Forma e ideología de Oficio de tinieblas de Rosario Castellanos," *Revista de Crítica Literaria Latinoamericana* 7–8, 1978, 80. See also A. Taylor, "El intelectual indigenista ficcionalizado e histórico en una novela de Rosario Castellanos: *Oficio de tinieblas,*" *Formaciones sociales e identidades culturales en la literatura hispanoamericana; ensayos en honor de Juan Armando Epple,* ed. Rosamel Benavides (Valdivia, Chile: Ediciones Barba de Palo, 1997), 215–228.

12. Alberto Moreiras, "The End of Magical Realism: José María Arguedas's Passionate Signifier," *The Exhaustion of Difference* (Durham, NC: Duke University Press, 2001), 185.

13. Ibid., 186–87.

14. Ibid., 194.

15. John Beverley, *Subalternity and Representation* (Durham, NC: Duke University Press, 1999), 47.

16. Joanna O'Connel, *Prospero's Daughter* (Austin: University of Texas Press, 1995), 60.

17. Moreiras, 194.

18. O'Connel, 62.

19. Sommer, *Proceed with Caution,* 3.

20. Ibid, xiii.

Chapter 4. Testimonio and Indigenous Struggles for Autonomy

1. For a broad introduction to contemporary indigenous-language authors in Mexico, see Carlos Montemayor and Donald Frischmann, *Words of the True Peoples: An Anthology of Contemporary Mexican Indigenous-Language Writers* (Austin: University of Texas Press, 2005).

2. Jacinto Arias Pérez, *El arreglo de los pueblos indios: la incansable tarea de reconstitución* (Mexico City: Secretaría de Educación Pública, 1994), 379–99.

3. Emilio García Riera and Fernando Macotela, *La guía del cine mexicano de la pantalla grande a la television, 1919–1984* (Mexico City: Editorial Patria, 1984), 295.

4. Political corruption, evidenced by the growing presence of *"acarreados"* (truckloads of "supporters" coerced into political participation by party and union bosses), as well as bald-faced electoral fraud at the ballot box, is well documented in the documentary *Mexico: The Frozen Revolution.* Dir. Raymundo Gleyzer (New York: Cinema Guild, 1987).

5. Thomas E. Skidmore and Peter H. Smith, *Modern Latin America* (New York: Oxford University Press, 2001), 248.

6. Subcomandante Insurgente Marcos and the Zapatista Army of National Liberation, *Shadows of Tender Fury.* Trans. and edited by Frank Bardacke, Leslie López, and the Watsonville, California Staff Human Rights Committee (New York: Monthly Review Press, 1995), 52.

7. Roger Bartra, *Las redes imaginarias del poder político* (Mexico City: Oceano, 1996).

8. John Beverley, *Against Literature* (Minneapolis: University of Minnesota Press, 1993),105.

Chapter 5. From Malinche to Matriarchal Utopia: Gendered and Sexualized Visions of Indigeneity

1. Beginning in the early 1970s, Isthmus Zapotec cultural production came to be synonymous with ethnic-political struggle for autonomy from the PRI, which had controlled municipal, state, and national politics for nearly seventy years. By 1981, a grassroots movement called the Coalition of Workers, Peasants, and Students of the Isthmus (Coalición Obrero Campesino Estudantil del Istmo; COCEI) led the first and only successful campaign to oust the PRI from municipal government. The popular government (*ayuntamiento popular*) pursued an ambitious course of socioeconomic and cultural transformation based on the restitution of peasant lands, use of the Zapotec language as the lingua franca of political struggle, and the nurturing of Isthmus Zapotec cultural and intellectual life. Along with this flowering of Isthmus Zapotec art and culture, Zapotec and non-Zapotec social scientists have sought to understand the historical and socioeconomic factors that lend credence to the pervasive myths of Isthmus Zapotec exceptionality. See Howard Campbell et al., *Zapotec Struggles: Histories, Politics and Representations from Juchitán, Oaxaca* (Washington D.C.: Smithsonian Institution Press, 1993); Campbell, *Zapotec Renaissance: Ethnic Politics and Cultural Revivalism in Southern Mexico* (Albuquerque: University of New Mexico Press, 1994); and Marinella Miano Borruso, *Hombre, mujer y muxe en el Istmo de Tehuantepec* (Mexico City: Plaza y Valdés, 2002) for in-depth discussions of the relationship between the COCEI movement and Isthmus Zapotec cultural production in the 1970s and 1980s.

2. For a timely analysis of women's participation and representation in national political arenas throughout the twentieth century in Mexico, see Victoria Rodríguez, *Women in Contemporary Mexican Politics* (Austin: University of Texas Press, 2003). For a theoretically and historically rich analysis of the intersections of gender identity and national identity in Mexico, see Estela Serret, "Identidad de género e identidad nacional en México" *La identitad nacional Mexican como problema politico y cultural* (Mexico City: Siglo XXI Editores, 1999).

3. According to Frances Karttunen, the multiple valences implied by the many names for doña Marina/Malintzin/Malinche stem from the different resonances she has among those who name her: "Her name, like her person, was handed back and forth and invested with multiple significances. When she was given to Hernando Cortés and his party in 1519, she received the baptismal name of Marina. Nahuatl speakers, who recognized no distinction between *r* and *l*, therefore addressed her reverentially as Malin-tzin. The Spaniards in turn heard Malinzin as Malinche, a name that in the course of Mexican history has become synonymous with selling out to foreigners. Yet to the old conqueror Bernal Díaz del Castillo, who made her the heroine of his account

of the conquest of Mexico, she was always 'doña Marina,' the respectful Spanish *doña* being the very equivalent of the Nahuatl honorific *-tzin*." "Rethinking Malinche," *Indian Women of Early Mexico* (Norman: University of Oklahoma Press, 1997), 14–15.

4. Translations in Campbell et al., 1993 by Cynthia Steele.

5. Hence, for Paz, the obsession with death, which is ritualized in the Day of the Dead, is actually an obsession with origin, with temporarily recapturing that part of "ourselves" that has been banished to "that cave or cellar in continuous somnolence and likewise in perpetual fermentation" (1985, 287). Paz argues that bringing that repressed element to consciousness for one magical day aids in the task of keeping it repressed the rest of the year. See Paz,47–64.

6. The U.S.-based Wal-Mart, the largest retailer in Mexico with revenues of over $13 billion a year, opened a new megastore in Juchitán under the name of Bodegas Aurrera. This comes on the heels of the opening of a Bodegas Aurrera in the largely Purépecha City of Pátzcuaro Michoacán and another one half a mile from the ancient Pyramids of Teotihuacan near Mexico City. See http://www.corpwatch.org/article.php?id=12589

Conclusion

1. Natividad Gutiérrez, *Nationalist Myths and Ethnic Identities: Indigenous Intellectuals and the Mexican State* (Lincoln: University of Nebraska Press, 1999).

2. Ernesto García Canclini, *Culturas híbridas: Estrategias para entrar y salir de la modernidad* (Mexico: Grijalbo, 1989). For a critique of the spatial and thematic organization of the National Museum of Anthropology, particularly how it enacts the "unification and centralization established by political nationalism in contemporary Mexico," see pp. 165–77.

3. Consuelo Sánchez, *Los pueblos indígenas: del indigenismo a la autonomía* (Mexico City: Siglo XXI, 1999), 102.

4. Gareth Williams, *The Other Side of the Popular: Neoliberalism and Subalternity in Latin America* (Durham, NC. Duke University Press, 2002).

5. Claudio Lomnitz, *Deep Mexico, Silent Mexico: An Anthropology of Nationalism* (Minneapolis: University of Minnesota Press, 2001).

6. Judith Amador and Columba Vértiz, "El INI convertido en oficina de gobierno," *Proceso* (June 2003):66–69.

7. Some of the pioneering critiques of *indigenismo* in Mexico include: Roger Bartra, *Estructura agraria y clases sociales en México* (Mexico City: Ediciones Era, 1974); Guillermo Bonfil Batalla et al., *De eso que llaman antropología mexicana* (Mexico City: Editorial Nuestro Tiempo, 1970); Pablo González Casanova, *La democracia en México* (Mexico City: Ediciones Era, 1965); Rodolfo Stavenhagen, *Las clases sociales en las sociedades agrarias* (Mexico City: Siglo XXI Editores, 1969).

8. Armando Bartra, "Sobrevivientes," *De fotógrafos y de indios* (Mexico City: Ediciones Tecolote, 2000).

9. Williams, *The Other Side of the Popular*, 174.

10. Martín Lienhard, "La noche de los Mayas: Indigenous Mesoamericans in Cinema and Literature, 1917–1943," *Journal of Latin American Cultural Studies* 13(1): 35–62.

11. Shannan Mattiace, *To See With Two Eyes: Peasant Activism and Indian Autonomy in Chiapas, Mexico* (Albuquerque: University of New Mexico Press, 2003), 16.

Bibliography

http://www.nodo50.org/pchiapas/chiapas/documentos/calenda/chiapas.htm

Abreu Gómez, Ermilo. *Canek y otras historias indias.* Buenos Aires: Ediciones López Negri, 1953.

Acta Final del Primer Congreso Indigenista Interamericano. Washington D.C.: Unión Panamericana, 1940. Conference Series 30.

Aguirre Beltrán, Gonzalo. *Obra antropológica VI: El proceso de aculturación y el cambio socio-cultural en México.* Mexico City: Fondo de Cultura Económica, 1992.

———. *Obra antropológica X: Teoría y práctica de la educación indígena.* Mexico City: Fondo de Cultura Económica, 1992.

———. *Obra antropológica XI: Obra polémica.* Mexico City: Fondo de Cultura Económica, 1992.

———. *Obra antropológica XII: Lenguas vernáculas.* Mexico City: Fondo de Cultura Económica, 1993.

Ahern, Maureen, ed. *A Rosario Castellanos Reader.* Austin: University of Texas Press, 1988.

Alcina Franch, José, ed. *Indianismo e indigenismo en América.* Madrid: Alianza Editorial, 1990.

Alonso, Ana María. "Conforming Disconformity: 'Mestizaje,' Hybridity, and the Aesthetics of Mexican Nationalism." *Cultural Anthropology* 19:4(2004): 459–90.

Amador, Judith, and Columba Vértiz. "El INI convertido en oficina de gobierno." *Proceso* (June 2003): 66–69.

Americas: Continent on the Move. Part 3. dirs. Raymond Telles and Marc de Beaufort. WGBH Educational Foundation, 1993.

Arguedas, José María. *Formación de una cultura nacional indoamericana.* Mexico City: Fondo de Cultura Económica, 1989.

Arias Pérez, Jacinto. *El arreglo de los pueblos indios: la incansable tarea de reconstitución.* Mexico City: Secretaría de Educación Pública, 1994.

Artís, Gloria, ed. *Encuentro de voces: la etnografía de México en el siglos XX.* Mexico: Instituto Nacional de Antropología e Historia, 2005.

Atkinson, Paul. *The Ethnographic Imagination: Textual Constructions of Reality.* New York: Routledge, 1990.

Bachillerato Integral Comunitario Ayuujk Polivalente. *La voz y la palabra del pueblo ayyujk.* Mexico: Porrua, 2001.

Baddeley, Oriana, and Valerie Frazer. *Drawing the Line: Art and Cultural Identity in Contemporary Latin America.* New York: Verso, 1989.

Bardacke, Frank. *Shadows of Tender Fury: The Letters and Communiques of Subcomandante Marcos and the Zapatista Army of National Liberation.* Trans. Leslie López, John Ross, and the Watsonville, California Staff Human Rights Committee. New York: Monthly Review Press, 1995.

Barnet, Miguel. *Biography of a Runaway Slave.* trans. Nick Hill. Willimantic, CT: Curbstone Press, 1994.

Barrios de Chungara, Domitila. Ed. Moema Viezzer. *Si Me permiten hablar: Testimonio de Domitila, una mujer de las minas de Bolivia.* Mexico City: Siglo XXI Editores, 1982.

Barry, Tom. *Zapata's Revenge: Free Trade and the Farm Crisis in Mexico.* Boston: South End Press, 1995.

Bartolomé, Miguel Alberto. *Gente de costumbre y gente de razón: las identidades étnicas en México.* Mexico City: Siglo XXI Editores, 1997.

Bartra, Armando, Alejandra Moreno Toscano, and Elisa Ramírez Castañeda. *De fotógrafos y de indios.* Mexico City: Ediciones Tecolote, 2000.

Bartra, Roger. *Las redes imaginarias del poder político.* Mexico City: Oceano, 1996.

Bartra, Roger, et al. *Caciquismo y poder politico en el México rural.* Mexico City: Siglo XXI Editores, 1975.

Bebbington, Anthony, et al. *Non-governmental Organizations and the State in Latin America: Rethinking Roles in Sustainable Agricultural Development.* New York: Routledge, 1993.

Bengoa, José. *La emergencia indígena en América Latina.* Mexico: Fondo de Cultura Económica, 2000.

Benjamin, Thomas L. "A Time of Reconquest: History, the Maya Revival, and the Zapatista Rebellion of Chiapas." *The American Historical Review* 105:2(2000).

———. "Passages to Leviathan: Chiapas and the Mexican State, 1891–1947." Ph.D. diss. Michigan State University, 1981.

Bernard, H. Russell, and Jesús Salinas Pedraza. *Native Ethnography.* Newbury Park, CA: Sage Publications, 1989.

Beverley, John. *Against Literature.* Minneapolis: University of Minnesota Press, 1993.

———. *Subalternity and Representation.* Durham, NC: Duke University Press, 1999.

Bigas Torres, Sylvia. *La narrativa indigenista mexicana del siglo XX.* Guadalajara, Mexico: Editorial Universidad de Guadalajara, 1990.

Blancarte, Roberto, ed. *Cultura e identidad nacional.* Mexico City: Fondo de Cultura Económica, 1994.

Blossoms of Fire. dir. Maureen Gosling. Oakland, CA: Intrépidas Productions, 2000.

Bonfil Batalla, Guillermo. *México Profundo: una civilización negada*. Mexico City: Grijalbo, 1994.

———, ed. *Nuevas identidades culturales en México*. Mexico City: Consejo Nacional Para la Cultura y las Artes, 1993.

Bourdieu, Pierre. *The Field of Cultural Production*. New York: Columbia University Press, 1993.

Brading, David. "Manuel Gamio and Official Indigenismo in Mexico." *Bulletin of Latin American Research* 7:1 (1988): 75–89.

Brice Heath, Shirley. *La política del lenguaje en México*. Mexico City: Universidad Nacional Autónoma de México, 1980.

Brushwood, John S. *Narrative Innovation and Political Change in Mexico*. New York: Peter Lang, 1989.

Burgos-Debray, Elizabeth. *Me llamo Rigoberta Menchú y así me nació la conciencia*. Siglo Veintiuno: México, 1985.

Burguete Cal y Mayor, Aracely. *Indigenous Autonomy in Mexico*. Copenhagen, Denmark: International Work Group for Indigenous Affairs, 2000.

Butler, Judith. *Gender Trouble: Feminism and the Subversion of Identity*. New York: Routledge, 1990.

Camayd-Freixas, Erik, and José Eduardo González, eds. *Primitivism and Identity in Latin America*. Tucson: The University of Arizona Press, 2000.

Campbell, Howard. *Zapotec Renaissance: Ethnic Politics and Cultural Revivalism in Southern Mexico*. Albuquerque: University of New Mexico Press, 1994.

Campbell, Howard, et al. *Zapotec Struggles: Histories, Politics and Representations from Juchitán, Oaxaca*. Washington D.C.: Smithsonian Institution Press, 1993.

Caso, Alfonso. "Definición del indio y lo indio." *América Indígena* 8:4 (October 1948): 1–2.

———. *Indigenismo*. México, Instituto Nacional Indigenista, 1958.

———. *Métodos y resultados de la política indigenista en México*. Mexico City: Instituto Nacional Indigenista, 1954.

Castañeda, Jorge G. *Utopia Unarmed: The Latin American Left after the Cold War*. New York: Vintage Books, 1994.

Castellanos, Rosario. *Balún canán*. Fondo de Cultura Económica: México, 1959.

———. *Ciudad Real*. Alfaguara: México, 1996.

———. *Meditación en el umbral*. Mexico City: Fondo de Cultura Económica, 1995.

———. *Oficio de tinieblas*. México: Juaquín Mortiz, 1962.

———. *El uso de la palabra*. Mexico City: Excelsior, 1974.

Castillo, Debra. *Easy Women: Sex and Gender in Modern Mexican Fiction*. Minneapolis: University of Minnesota Press, 1998.

Castro, Carlo Antonio. *Los hombres verdaderos*. Xalapa, Mexico: Universidad Veracruzana, 1959.

Cevallos, Diego. "Mexico: Wal-Mart's Plans for Indigenous Areas under Fire." August 25, 2005. http://www.corpwatch.org/article.php?id=12589 (accessed Jan 15, 2007).

Chiñas, Beverly. *The Isthmus Zapotecs: Women's Roles in Cultural Context.* New York: Holt, Rinehart and Winston, 1973.

Comandante Esther. "Mensaje central del EZLN ante el Congreso de la Unión." http://www.eocities.com/tierraylibertad_ac/indigenas/cdtaesther.htm (accessed Oct. 23, 2008).

Cornejo Polar, Antonio. "El indigenismo y las literaturas heterogéneas: su doble estatuto sociocultural." *Revista de Crítica Literaria Latinoamericana* 7–8, 1978.

———. *Sobre literatura y crítica literaria latinoamericanas.* Caracas: Universidad Central de Venezuela, 1982.

Coronado, Gabriela, and Bob Hodge. *El hipertexto multicultural en México postmoderno: Paradojas e incertidumbres.* Mexico: Porrua, 2004.

Cowie, Lancelot. *El indio en la narrativa contemporánea de México y de Guatemala.* Trans. María Elena Hope Sánchez Mejorada. Mexico City: Instituto Nacional indigenista, 1976.

Dalsimer, Katherine. *Female Adolescence: Psychoanalytic Reflections on Works of Literature.* New Haven, CT: Yale University Press, 1986.

Dawson, Alexander S. *Indian and Nation in Revolutionary Mexico.* Tucson: University of Arizona Press, 2004.

Deleuze, Gilles, and Félix Guattari. *Kafka: Toward a Minor Literature.* Trans. Dana Polan. University of Minnesota Press: Minneapolis, 1986.

———. *A Thousand Plateaus.* Trans. Brian Massumi. University of Minnesota Press: Minneapolis, 1987.

De Valdéz, María Elena. *The Shattered Mirror: Representations of Women in Mexican Literature.* Austin: The University of Texas Press, 1998.

De Vos, Jan. *Una tierra para sembrar sueños: historia reciente de la selva lacandona, 1950–2000.* Mexico: Fondo de Cultura Económica, 2002.

Díaz Polanco, Héctor. *Autonomía regional: la autodeterminación de los pueblos indios.* Mexico City: Siglo XXI Editores, 1996.

———. *El canon Snorri: Diversidad cultural y tolerancia.* Mexico: Universidad de la Ciudad de México, 2004.

———. *Indigenismo, modernización y marginalidad.* Mexico City: Juan Pablos Editores, 1987.

Dieckhoff, Alain, and Natividad Gutiérrez. *Modern Roots: Studies of National Identity.* Burlington, VT: Ashgate, 2001.

Domenella, Ana Rosa, et al. *Medio siglo de literatura latinoamericana: 1945–1995.* vols. 1 & 2. Mexico City: Universidad Autónoma Metropolitana, 1997.

Dominguez Micheal, Christopher. *Antología de la narrativa mexicana del siglo XX.* Mexico City: Fondo de Cultura Económica, 1991.

Doremus, Anne T. *Culture, Politics and National Identity in Mexican Literature and Film, 1929–1952.* New York: Peter Lang, 2001.

Eagleton, Terry. *Literary Theory*. Minneapolis: University of Minnesota Press, 1983.

EZLN: *Documentos y comunicados*. Prologue By Antonio García de León. Commentary by Carlos Monsiváis and Elena Poniatowska. Mexico: Ediciones Era, 1994. Vols 1–3.

EZLN and subcomandante Marcos. *Crónicas intergalácticas: Primer Encuentro Intercontinental por la Humanidad y Contra el Neoliberalismo*. Chiapas, Mexico: Planeta Tierra, 1997.

Fass Emery, Amy. *The Anthropological Imagination in Latin American Literature*. Columbia: University of Missourri Press, 1996.

Favre, Henri. *Cambio y continuidad entre los mayas de México*. Mexico City: Fondo de Cultura Económica, 1971.

Ferhrenbach, T. R. *Fire and Blood: A History of Mexico*. New York: Da Capo Press, 1995.

Florescano, Enrique, ed. *Mitos mexicanos*. Mexico City: Alfaguara, 1995.

———. *El patrimonio cultural de México*. Mexico City: Fondo de Cultura Económica, 1993.

Flores Magón, Ricardo. *Regeneración: 1910–1918*. Mexico City: Ediciones Era, 1997.

Foster, David William, ed. *Mexican Literature: A History*. Austin: University of Texas Press, 1994.

Franco, Jean. *An Introduction to Spanish American Literature*. New York: Cambridge University Press, 1994.

———. "La Malinche y el primer mundo." *La Malinche, sus padres y sus hijos*, ed. Margo Glanz. Mexico City: Taurus (2001): 201–17.

Friedlander, Judith. *Being Indian in Hueyapan: A Study of Forced Identity in Contemporary Mexico*. New York: St. Martin's Press, 1975.

Gamio, Manuel. *Forjando Patria*. Mexico City: Porrua, [1916] 1960.

García Canclini, Néstor. *Culturas híbridas: Estrategias para entrar y salir de la modernidad*. Mexico City: Grijalbo, 1989.

———. *Transforming Modernity: Popular Culture in Mexico*. trans. Lidia Lozano. Austin: University of Texas Press, 1993.

García de León, Antonio. *Resistencia y utopia*. Mexico City: Ediciones Era, 1998.

García Mora, Carlos and Andrés Medina, eds. *La quiebra política de la antropología social en México*. México: UNAM, 1986.

García Riera, Emilio, and Fernando Macotela. *La guía del cine mexicano de la pantalla grande a la televisión, 1919–1984*. Mexico City: Editorial Patria, 1984.

Gómez, Magdalena. "¿Indigenismo del cambio?" *La Jornada* (May 2003).

Gómez Gutiérrez, Domingo. *Jwan Lopes Bats'il Ajaw/Juan López, héroe tzaltal*. Mexico City: Instituto Nacional Indigenista, 1996.

González Casanova, Pablo. *La democracia en México*. Mexico City: Ediciones Era, 1965.

————. *Sociología de la explotación.* Mexico City: Siglo XXI Editores, 1987.

Gossen, Gary H. *Telling Maya Tales: Tzotzil Identities in Modern Mexico.* New York: Routledge, 1999.

Gould, Jeffrey L. *To Die in this Way: Nicaraguan Indians and the Myth of Mestizaje, 1880–1965.* Durham, NC: Duke University Press, 1998.

Graham, Richard, et al. *The Idea of Race in Latin America, 1870–1940.* Austin: University of Texas Press, 1990.

Gramsci, Antonio. *Selections from the Prison Notebooks.* Trans. Quintin Hoare and Geoffrey Nowell Smith. New York: International Publishers, 1997.

Greenberg, James B. *Blood Ties: Life and Violence in Rural Mexico.* Tucson: University of Arizona Press, 1989.

Griffin, Mark Odell. "Dialoguing with the Discourse of the Nation: The Mexican Revolution and the 'Cosmic Race' in the Indigenista Narrative of Chiapas." Ph.D. diss. Tulane University, 1996.

Gruzinski, Serge. *Images at War.* Trans. Heather MacLean. Durham, NC: Duke University Press, 2001.

Gugelberger, Georg M., ed. *The Real Thing: Testimonial Discourse and Latin America.* Durham, NC: Duke University Press, 1996.

Guha, Ranajit, and Gayatri Chakravorty Spivak. *Selected Subaltern Studies.* New York: Oxford University Press, 1988.

Gutierrez, Natividad. *Nationalist Myths and Ethnic Identities: Indigenous Intellectuals and the Mexican State.* Lincoln: University of Nebraska Press, 1999.

Hamilton, Nora. *The Limits of State Autonomy: Post-Revolutionary Mexico.* Princeton, NJ: Princeton University Press, 1982.

Hayden, Tom, ed. *The Zapatista Reader.* New York: Thunder's Mouth Press/ Nation Books, 2002.

Henríquez Ureña, Pedro. *Literary Currents in Hispanic America.* Cambridge, MA: Harvard University Press, 1945.

Hernández Castillo, R. Aída. *Histories and Stories from Chiapas: Border Identities in Southern Mexico.* Trans. Martha Pou. Austin: University of Texas Press, 2001.

Hernández Navarro, Luis, and Ramón Vera Herrera, comps. *Acuerdos de San Andrés.* Mexico City: Editorial Era, 1998.

Hewitt de Alcántara, Cynthia. *Anthropological Perspectives on Rural Mexico.* Boston: Routledge & Kegan Paul, 1984.

Higgins, Nicholas P. *Understanding the Chiapas Rebellion: Modernist Visions and the Invisible Indian.* Austin: University of Texas Press, 2004.

Hofstadter, Dan. *Mexico 1946–73.* New York: Facts on File, 1974.

Jackson, Micheal. *Minima Ethnographica: Intersubjectivity and the Anthropological Project.* Chicago: The University of Chicago Press, 1998.

Jameson, Fredric. "Criticism in History." *Criticism: Major Statements.* Ed. Charles Kaplan and William Anderson. New York: St. Martin's Press, 1991.

————. *The Political Unconscious.* Ithaca, NY: Cornell University Press, 1981.

————. *Postmodernism, or the Cultural Logic of Late Capitalism.* Durham, NC: Duke University Press, 1991.

Joseph, Gilbert M., and Daniel Nugent, eds. *Everyday Forms of State Formation: Revolution and the Negotiation of Rule in Modern Mexico.* Durham, NC: Duke University Press, 1994.

Kadir, Djelal. *The Other Writing: Postcolonial Essays in Latin America's Writing Culture.* West Lafayette, IN: Purdue University Press, 1993.

Karttunen, Frances. "Rethinking Malinche." *Indian Women of Early Mexico.* Ed. Susan Schroeder, Stephanie Wood, and Robert Haskett. Norman: University of Oklahoma Press, 1997, 291–312.

Katzenberger, Elaine, ed. *First World, Ha Ha Ha! The Zapatista Challenge.* San Francisco, CA: City Lights Books, 1995.

Kicza, John E. *The Indian in Latin American History.* Wilmington, DE: Scholarly Resources, Inc., 1993.

Krauze, Enrique. *Mexico: Biography of Power.* Trans. Hank Heifetz. New York: Harper Collins, 1997.

Krotz, Esteban. *La otredad cultural entre utopia y ciencia.* Mexico: Fondo de Cultura Económica, 2002.

La Botz, Dan. *Democracy in Mexico: Peasant Rebellion and Political Reform.* Boston: South End Press, 1995.

Laclau, Ernesto, and Chantal Mouffe. *Hegemony and Socialist Strategy: Towards a Radical Democratic Politics.* New York: Verso, 1996.

Langford, Walter M. *The Mexican Novel Comes of Age.* Notre Dame, IN: University of Notre Dame Press, 1971.

Larsen, Neil. *Reading North by South.* Minneapolis: University of Minnesota Press, 1995.

Las Casas, Bartolomé de. *Brevísima relación de la destruccion de las Indias.* Madrid: Cátedra, 1991.

Lenkersdorf, Carlos, ed. *Indios somos con orgullo: poesía maya-tojolabal.* Mexico City: Universidad Nacional Autónoma de México, 1999.

————. *Los hombres verdaderos: voces y testimonios tojolabales.* México: Siglo XXI Editores, 1996.

León Portilla, Miguel, ed. *Motivos de la antropología americanista: indagaciones en la diferencia.* Mexico City: Fondo de Cultura Económica, 2001.

————. ed.*Visión de los vencidos.* México: UNAM, 1959.

León Portilla, Miguel, et al., eds. *In the Language of Kings: An Anthology of Mesoamerican Literature, Pre-colombian to the Present.* New York: Norton, 2001.

Lewis, Diane. "Anthropology and Colonialism." *Current Anthropology* 14, 5 (December 1973).

Lewis, Oscar. *The Children of Sánchez.* New York: Basic Books, 1969.

Leyva Solano, Xochitl, and Gabriel Ascencio Flores. *Lacandonia al filo del agua.* Mexico: Fondo de Cultura Económica, 2002.

Lienhard, Martín. La noche de los Mayas: Indigenous Mesoamericans in

Cinema and Literature, 1917–1943. *Journal of Latin American Cultural Studies* 13:1(2004): 35–62.

———. *La voz y su huella.* Hanover, NH: Ediciones del Norte, 1991.

Lindstrom, Naomi. *The Social Conscience of Latin American Writing.* Austin: University of Texas Press, 1998.

Lomnitz, Claudio. *Deep Mexico, Silent Mexico: An Anthropology of Nationalism.* Minneapolis: University of Minnesota Press, 2001.

———. *Modernidad indiana: nueve ensayos sobre nación y mediación en México.* Mexico City: Planeta, 1999.

Lomnitz-Adler, Claudio. *Exits from the Labyrinth: Culture and Ideology in the Mexican National Space.* Berkeley: University of California Press, 1992.

López, Miguel. "(De) generando heterogeneidades: relecturas femeninas del mestizaje en la novela indigenista Mexicana." Ph.D. diss, University of California, Berkeley, 1998.

López-Baralt, Mercedes. *Para decir al otro: literatura y antropología en nuestra América.* Madrid: Iberoamericana, 2005.

López González, Aralia. *La espiral parece un círculo: la narrativa de Rosario Castellanos.* Mexico City: Universidad Autónoma Metropolitana, 1991.

López y Fuentes, Gregorio. *El Indio.* New York: Norton & Company, 1940.

López y Rivas, Gilberto. *Nación y pueblos indios en el neoliberalismo.* México: Plaza y Váldes Editores, 1995.

Macherey, Pierre. *A Theory of Literary Production.* Trans. Geoffrey Wall. Routledge: New York, 1986.

Magdaleno, Mauricio. *El resplandor.* Mexico City: Espasa-Calpe, 1937.

Maldonado Alvarado, Benjamín. *Los indios en las aulas: dinámica de dominación y resistencia en Oaxaca.* Mexico: Instituto Nacional de Antropología e Historia, 2002.

Manuel, George, and Michael Posluns. *The Fourth World: An Indian Reality.* Free Press: New York, 1974.

Marcos, subcomandante Insurgente. "Chiapas: La treceava estela" http://www.margen.org/desdeelmargen/num4/estela.html (accessed Jan 15, 2007).

Mariátegui, José Carlos. *Siete ensayos de interpretación de la realidad peruana.* Mexico City: Ediciones Era, 1993.

Marion, Marie Odile. *Entre anhelos y recuerdos.* Mexico City: Plaza y Valdéz, 1997.

Martínez, José Luis, and Christopher Dominguez Micheal. *La literatura mexicana del siglo XX.* Mexico City: Consejo Nacional Para la Cultura y las Artes, 1995.

Marx, Carl. *The Eighteenth Brumaire of Louis Bonaparte.* New York: International Publishers, 1963.

Marzal, Manuel. *Historia de la antropología. Vol.1 Antropología indigenista.* Quito: Abya Yala, 1998.

Masera Cerutti, Omar. *Crisis y mecanizacion de la agricultura campesina.* Mexico City: El Colegio de México, 1990.

Máynez, Pilar. *Lenguas y literaturas indígenas en el México contemporáneo.* Mexico: Universidad Autónoma de México, 2003.

Medina, Andrés, and Carlos García Mora. *La quiebra política de la antropología social en México.* Mexico City: Universidad Nacional Autónoma de México, 1983.

Men with Guns. Dir. John Sayles. Culver City, CA: Columbia Tristar Pictures, 1998.

Meneses Velázquez, Marina. "El camino de ser mujer en Juchitán." *Juchitán, la ciudad de las mujeres.* Ed. Veronika Bennholdt-Thomsen. Oaxaca: Instituto Oaxaqeño de las Culturas, 1997, 99–163.

Mexico: The Frozen Revolution. Dir. Raymundo Gleyzer. New York: Cinema Guild, 1987.

Miano Borruso, Marinella. *Hombre, mujer y mux' en el Istmo de Tehuantepec.* Mexico City: Plaza y Valdés, 2002.

Middlebrook, Kevin J. *The Paradox of Revolution: Labor, the State and Authoritarianism in Mexico.* Baltimore: The Johns Hopkins University Press, 1995.

Montemayor, Carlos. "Adiós al INI." *La Jornada* (May, 2003).

———. *Arte y plegaria en las lenguas indígenas de México.* Mexico City: Fondo de Cultura Económica, 1999.

———. *Arte y trama en el cuento indígena.* Mexico City: Fondo de Cultura Económica, 1998.

———. *Chiapas: la rebelión indígena de México.* Mexico City: Joaquín Mortíz, 1997.

———. *Guerra en el paraíso.* Mexico: Diana literaria, 1991.

———. *Situación actual y perspectivas de la literatura en lenguas indígenas.* Mexico City: Consejo Nacional para la Cultura y las Artes, 1993.

Montemayor, Carlos, ed. *Los Escritores Indígenas actuales.* Mexico City: Consejo Nacional para la Cultura y las Artes, 1992. vols. 1 & 2.

Montemayor, Carlos, and Donald Frischmann, eds. *Words of the True Peoples Palabras de los seres verdaderos: Anthology of Contemporary Mexican Indigenous Language Writers.* Austin: University of Texas Press, 2004.

Morales Bermúdez, Jesús. *Antigua palabra: Narrativa indígena ch'ol.* Mexico City: Plaza y Valdéz Editores, 1999.

———. *Aproximaciones a la poesía y la narrativa de Chiapas.* San Cristóbal de las Casas, Chiapas, Mexico: Universidad de Ciencias y Artes del Estado de Chiapas, 1997.

———. *Memorial del tiempo o vía de las conversaciones.* Mexico City: Editorial Katun, 1987.

Morales Bermúdez, Jesús, et al. *La tierra en Chiapas: viejos problemas nuevos.* Mexico City: Plaza y Valdéz, 1999.

Moraña, Mabel. *Angel Rama y los estudios latinoamericanos.* Pittsburgh: University of Pittsburgh Press, 1997.

Moreiras, Alberto. *The Exhaustion of Difference: The Politics of Latin American Cultural Studies*. Durham, NC: Duke University Press, 2001.

Moscoso Pastrana, Prudencio. *Rebeliones indígenas en los altos de Chiapas*. México: UNAM, 1992.

Napolitano, Valentina, and Xochitl Leyva Solano, eds. *Encuentros antropológicos: Power, Identity and Mobility in Mexican Society*. London: University of London Institute of Latin American Studies, 1998.

Nash, June C. *Mayan Visions: the Quest for Autonomy in an Age of Globalization*. New York: Routledge, 2001.

Nelson, Diane M. *A Finger in the Wound: Body Politics in Quincentennial Guatemala*. Berkeley: University of California Press, 1999.

Niblo, Stephen R. *Mexico in the 1940s: Modernity, Politics, Corruption*. Wilmington, DE: Scholarly Resources Inc., 1999.

Nuñez Loyo, Verónica. *Crisis y redefinición del indigenismo en México*. Mexico: Instituto Mora, 2004.

O'Connel, Joanna. *Prospero's Daughter: The Prose of Rosario Castellanos*. Austin: The University of Texas Press, 1995.

Olivé Negrete, Julio César. *Antropología mexicana*. Mexico: Plaza y Valdéz, 2000.

Ortiz, Fernando. *Contrapunteo cubano del tabaco y el azúcar*. Caracas: Biblioteca Ayacucho, 1987.

Otero, Gerardo, ed. *Neoliberalism Revisited: Economic Restructuring and Mexico's Political Future*. Boulder, CO: Westview Press, 1996.

Ovalle Fernández, Ignacio. "De la aldea al mundo." *Indigenismo: 40 años*. México: Instituto Nacional Indigenista, 1988.

———. *INI 30 años después: Revisión crítica*. México: México Indígena, 1978.

Paz, Octavio. *Labyrinth of Solitude and Other Writings*. Trans. Lysander Kemp, Yara Milos, and Rachel Phillips Belash. New York: Grove Press, 1985.

Pérez López, Enrique. "Religions Amongst Indigenous People of Today." *Aboriginal Voices*. 5:1(1998): 34–35.

Persons, Stow. *Ethnic Studies at Chicago: 1905–45*. Urbana: University of Illinois Press, 1987.

Pitarch Ramón, Pedro. *Ch'ulel: una etnografía de las almas tzeltales*. Mexico City: Fondo de Cultura Económica, 1996.

Poniatowska, Elena. *Hasta no verte Jesús mío*. Mexico City: Ediciones Era, 1969.

———. "Juchitán, a Town of Women," *Zapotec Struggles: Histories, Politics, and Representations from Juchitán, Oaxaca*. Campbell et al. Trans. Cynthia Steele. Washington D.C.: Smithsonian Institution Press, 1993, 133–35.

———. *La noche de Tlatelolco: testimonios de historia oral*. Mexico City: Ediciones Era, 1971.

———. *Luz y luna, las lunitas*. Mexico City: Ediciones Era, 1994.

Poniatowska, Elena, and Germán Dehesa. *México Indio: testimonios en blanco y negro*. Mexico City: Inverméxico, 1994.

Pozas, Ricardo. *Chamula*. Mexico City: Instituto Nacional Indigenista, Vol 1, 1979.

———. *Juan Pérez Jolote*. Mexico City: Fondo de Cultura Económica, 1952.

Pozas, Ricardo, and Isabel Horcasitas de Pozas. *Los indios en las clases sociales de México*. Mexico City: Siglo XXI Editores, 1976.

Pratt, Mary Louise. *Travel Writing and Transculturation*. New York: Routledge, 1992.

Prieto, René. *Body of Writing: Figuring Desire in Spanish American Literature*. Durham, NC: Duke University Press, 2000.

¡Que viva México! dir. Segei Eisenstein. New York: IFEX Films, 1979 (1932).

Quintana, María Esther. "Heterogeneidad cultural y conflicto en *Balún Canán* y *Oficio de Tinieblas* de Rosario Castellanos." *La seducción de la escritura: los discursos de la cultura hoy, 1996*. Rosaura Hernández Monroy and Maunuel F. Medina, eds. Mexico City: Fideicomiso para la Cultura México-Estados Unidos, 1997.

Rabasa, José. "Of Zapatismo: Reflections on the folkloric and the Impossible in a Subaltern Insurrection." *The Politics of Culture in the Shadow of Capital*. Lisa Lowe and David Lloyd, eds. Durham, NC: Duke University Press, 1997.

Ramírez Castañeda, Elisa. *La educación indígena en México*. Mexico: Universidad Nacional Autónoma de México, 2006.

Rama, Angel. *La ciudad letrada*. Hanover, NH: Ediciones del Norte, 1984.

———. *La novela en América Latina*. Xalapa, Mexico: Universidad Veracruzana, 1986.

———. *La transculturación narrativa en América Latina*. Mexico City: Siglo XXI Editores, 1982.

Ramos, Julio. *Desencuentros de la modernidad en América Latina: literatura y política en el siglo XIX*. Mexico City: Fondo de Cultura Económica, 1989.

Redfield, Robert. *Folk Cultures of the Yucatán*. Chicago: University of Chicago Press, 1948.

Revueltas, José. *Human Mourning*. Trans. Roberto Crespi. Minneapolis: University of Minnesota Press, 1989.

Riefler Bricker, Victoria. *The Indian Christ, the Indian King: The Historical Substrate of Maya Myth and Ritual*. Austin: University of Texas Press, 1981.

Rochfort, Desmond. *Mexican Muralists: Orozco, Rivera, Siqueiros*. San Francisco, CA: Chronicle Books, 1993.

Rodríguez, Victoria. *Women in Contemporary Mexican Politics*. Austin: University of Texas Press, 2003.

Rodríguez Chicharro, César. *Estudios de la literatura mexicana*. Mexico City: Universidad Autónoma de México, 1983.

Rojas González, Francisco. *El diosero*. Mexico City: Fondo de Cultura Económica, [1952] 1985.

———. *Lola Casanova*. Mexico City: Fondo de Cultura Económica, [1947] 1984.

Ros Romero, Consuelo. *La imágen del indio en el discurso del Instituto Nacional Indigenista*. México: Centro de Investigaciones y Estudios Superiores de Antropología Social, 1992.

Rosser, Harry L. *Conflict and Transition in Rural Mexico: The Fiction of Social Realism*. Waltham, MA: African Studies Association, 1980.

Rovira, Guiomar. *Mujeres de maíz: la voz de las indígenas de Chiapas y la rebelión Zapatista*. Mexico City: Ediciones Era, 2000.

Rubín, Ramon. *El callado dolor de los tzotziles*. Mexico City: Fondo de Cultura Económica, 1990.

Rulfo, Juan. *El llano en llamas*. Mexico City: Fondo de Cultura Económica, 1986.

Rulfo, Juan, et al. *Inframundo*. Hanover, N.H.: Ediciones del Norte, 1983.

Rus, Jan, Rosalva Aída Hernández Castillo, and Shannan L. Mattiace, eds. *Mayan Lives, Mayan Utopias: The Indigenous Peoples of Chiapas and the Zapatista Rebellion*. New York: Rowman and Littlefield, 2003.

Said, Edward W. *Orientalism*. New York: Vintage Books, 1979.

———. *Representations of the Intellectual*. New York: Vintage Books, 1994.

Saintoul, Catherine. *Racismo, etnocentrismo y literatura: la novela indigenista andina*. Buenos Aires: Ediciones del Sol, 1988.

Saldaña-Portillo, María Josefina. *The Revolutionary Imagination in the Americas and the Age of Development*. Durham, NC: Duke University Press, 2003.

Sánchez, Consuelo. *Los pueblos indígenas: del indigenismo a la autonomía*. Mexico City: Siglo XXI Editores, 1999.

Schmidt, Donald L. "Changing Narrative Techniques in the Mexican Indigenista Novel." Ph. D. diss., University of Kansas, 1972.

Serret, Estela. "Identidad de género e identidad nacional en México." *La identidad nacional mexicana como problema politico y cultural*, ed. Raul Bejar and Héctor Rosales. Mexico City: Siglo XXI Editores, 1999, 240–75.

Sierra, Justo. *The Political Evolution of the Mexican People*. Trans. Charles Ramsdell. Austin: University of Texas Press, 1969.

Skidmore, Thomas E. *Black into White: Race and Nationality in Brazilian Thought*. Durham, NC: Duke University Press, 1993.

Skidmore, Thomas E., and Peter H. Smith. *Modern Latin America*. New York: Oxford University Press, 2001.

Solís, Felipe, et al., eds. *Museo Nacional de la Antropología*. Mexico: Instituto Nacional de Antropología e Historia, 2004.

Sommer, Doris. *Foundational Fictions: The National Romances of Latin America*. Berkeley: University of California Press, 1991.

———. *Proceed with Caution, When Engaged by Minority Writing in the Americas*. Cambridge, MA: Harvard University Press, 1999.

Sommers, Joseph, "Forma e ideología de *Oficio de Tinieblas* de Rosario Castellanos." *Revista de Crítica Literaria Latinoamericana* 7–8 (1978).

————. *After the Storm: Landmarks in the Modern Mexican Novel.* Albuquerque: University of New Mexico Press, 1968.

Speed, Shannon, Rosalva Aída Hernández Castillo, and Lynn Stephen, eds. *Dissident Women: Gender and Cultural Politics in Chiapas.* Austin: University of Texas Press, 2006.

Spitta, Silvia. *Between Two Waters: Narratives of Transculturation in Latin America.* Houston: Rice University Press, 1995.

Spivak, Gayatri Chakravorty. *Outside in the Teaching Machine.* New York: Routledge, [1990] 1998.

Stavenhagen, Rodolfo. "Clases, colonialismo y aculturación." *Cuadernos del Seminario de Integración Sociál Guatemalteco* 19 (1968).

————. *Sociología y subdesarollo.* Mexico City: Nuestro Tiempo, 1971.

Steele, Cynthia. "Indigenismo y posmodernidad: narrativa indigenista, testimonio, teatro campesino y video en el Chiapas finisecular." *Revista de Crítica Literaria Latinoamericana* 19:38 (July–December 1993).

————. *La narrativa indigenista en los Estados Unidos y México.* Mexico City: Instituto Nacional Indigenista, 1986.

————. *Politics, Gender and the Mexican Novel, 1968–1988: Beyond the Pyramid.* Austin: University of Texas Press, 1992.

Stephen, Lynn. *¡Zapata Lives! Histories and Cultural Politics in Southern Mexico.* Berkeley: University of California Press, 2002.

Taussig, Michael. *Mimesis and Alterity: A Particular History of the Senses.* New York: Routledge, 1993.

Taylor, Analisa. "Between Official and Extra-official Indigenismos in Post-revolutionary Mexican Literature (1935–1950)." *Latin American Literary Review* 31:62 (July–December 2003): 96–119.

————. "The Ends of Indigenismo in Mexico." *Journal of Latin American Cultural Studies* 14: 1 (March 2005): 75–86.

————. "El intelectual indigenista ficcionalizado e histórico en una novela de Rosario Castellanos: *Oficio de tinieblas.*" Ed. Rosamel Benavides. *Formaciones sociales e identidades culturales en la literatura hispanoamericana.* Valdivia, Chile: Ediciones Barba de Palo, 1997.

————. "Malinche and Matriarchal Utopia: Gendered Visions of Indigeneity in Mexico." *Signs: Journal of Women in Culture and Society* 31:3 (Spring 2006).

Trigo, Benigno. *Subjects of Crisis: Race and Gender as Disease in Latin America.* Durham, NC: Duke University Press, 2000.

Tuhiwai Smith, Linda. *Decolonizing Methodologies: Research and Indigenous Peoples.* New York: Zed Books, 2004.

Underiner, Tamara. *Contemporary Theater in Mayan Mexico: Death-defying Acts.* Austin: University of Texas Press, 2004.

Van Cott, Donna Lee, ed. *Indigenous Peoples and Democracy in Latin America.* New York: St. Martin's Press, 1994.

Van der Haar, Gemma, and Carlos Lenkersdorf, eds. *San Miguel Chiptik: Testimonios de una comunidad tojolabal.* Mexico City: Siglo XXI Editores, 1998.

Vasconcelos, José. *The Cosmic Race/La raza cósmica.* Baltimore: The Johns Hopkins University Press, 1997

Vázquez Valle, Irene, ed. *La cultura popular vista por las elites.* México: UNAM, 1989.

Vellinga, Menno, ed. *The Changing Role of the State in Latin America.* Boulder, CO: Westview Press, 1998.

Villoro, Luis. *Los grandes momentos del indigenismo en México.* Mexico City: El Colegio de México, 1950.

Viqueira Albán, Juan Pedro. *Indios rebeldes e idólatras: dos ensayos históricos sobre la rebelión india de Cancuc, Chiapas, acaecida en el año 1712.* Mexico City: CIESAS, 1997.

————. *María de la candelaria, india natural de cancúc.* Mexico City: Fondo de Cultura Económica, 1993.

Vizcaíno, Fernando. *El nacionalismo mexicano en los tiempos de la globalización y el multiculturalismo.* Mexico: Universidad Nacional Autónoma de México, 2004.

Warman, Arturo. *Los indios mexicanos en el umbral del milenio.* Mexico: Fondo de Cultura Económica, 2003.

Warman, Arturo, et al. *De eso que llaman antropología mexicana.* Mexico City: Nuestro Tiempo, 1971.

Warnock, John. *The Other Mexico.* New York: Black Rose Books, 1995.

Weinberg, Bill. *Homage to Chiapas: New Indigenous Struggles in Mexico.* New York: Verso, 2000.

Williams, Gareth. *The Other Side of the Popular: Neoliberalism and Subalternity in Latin America.* Durham, NC: Duke University Press, 2002.

Williams, Raymond. *The Country and the City.* New York: Oxford University Press, 1975.

————. *Marxism and Literature.* New York: Oxford University Press, 1977.

Womack, Craig S. *Red on Red: Native American Literary Separatism.* Minneapolis: University of Minnesota Press, 1999.

Womack, John Jr. *Rebellion in Chiapas.* New York: The New Press, 1999.

Woodrich, Wendy Z. "Aspectos teóricos de la autobiografía y el testimonio femenino hispanoamericano: las historias de vida de Jesusa Palancares y Rigoberta Menchú." *El testimonio femenino como escritura contestataria.* Ed. Emma Sepúlveda Pulvirenti. Santiago, Chile: Ediciones Asterión, 1995.

Yúdice, George. *The Expediency of Culture: Uses of Culture in the Global Era.* Durham, NC: Duke University Press, 2003.

Zepeda, Eraclio. *Benzulul.* Xalapa, Mexico: Universidad Veracruzana, 1981.

Index

acculturation, 18–19, 52–53, 75. *See also Oficio de tinieblas*
activists, indigenous, 23
Alvarado, Benjamin Maldonado, 16
anthropologists, 13, 15, 20, 41–42, 70, 77
anthropology, 13, 19, 20, 109; applied, 44
Arguedas, José María, 63
assimilation, 9, 14, 35, 44, 46, 107, 112; partial, 45. *See also* incorporation
authorship, problem of, 76

Bartra, Roger, 118n10
Batalla, Guillermo Bonfil, 20
Beltrán, Gonzalo Aguirre, 18
Bermúdez, Jesús Morales, 10, 73–74
Beverley, John, 63, 80
Bigas Torres, Sylvia, 48
biography. *See Juan Pérez Jolote*
Blossoms of Fire (film), 82–84, 86–89, 103

Calderón, Felipe, 5, 114
Calles, Elías, 17
Camacho, Ávila, 40
capitalism, 62; transnational, 109
Caracoles, 79
Cárdenas, Lázaro, 14, 16–17, 40, 58
Caso, Alfonso, 4, 18, 19
Castellanos, Rosario, 9–10, 43, 55. *See also Oficio de tinieblas*
Castro, Carlo Antonio, 9, 39–41, 49, 50, 53
Chamula (Pozas), 46
Chamulan culture, 45–48. *See also Juan Pérez Jolote; Oficio de tinieblas*
Chiapas, 79
Chicharro, César Rodríguez, 53
Chingada, 94–95

Ch'ol community, 73–74
citizenship, 103–4; cultural metaphors for, 96, 102
CNC. *See* National Peasant Confederation
coming-of-age stories. *See* ethnographic coming-of-age stories; *Los hombres verdaderos*
communal land tenure system. *See ejido*
Consejo Nacional para el Desarollo de los Pueblos Indígenas (CONADEPI). *See* National Council for the Development of Indigenous Communities
Constitutional Article 27, 5–6
Cornejo Polar, Antonio, 64
corruption, 48
Cortés, Hernán, 85, 92, 97, 100
Cortés and Malinche (Orozco), 97–98
"cripples" (in literature), 31
"Cultural Diversity in Mexico," 105–8; map, 106
cultural metaphors for citizenship, 96, 102
cultural relativism, 41
culture, "national," 109

Davis, Kate, 86–87
Dawson, Alexander S., 14
dependency, 19
diversity map, 106

economy, "national," 109
Eisenstein, Sergei, 87
ejido, 17
El indio (López y Fuentes), 28–29
El resplandor (Magdaleno), 31–34
empowerment, 7, 22, 85, 115. *See also under* women

Entre anhelos y recuerdos (Marión), 10, 75–77
erotic utopia, 87
eroticism/sexuality, 34, 56, 84, 85
erotics and politics, relationship between, 34
Escuela Nacional de Antropología e Historia (ENAH). *See* National School of Anthropology and History
Esther, Comandante, 1, 103, 104
ethnographic coming-of-age stories, 39, 42–43, 46–47, 65–66. *See also Juan Pérez Jolote; Oficio de tinieblas*
ethnography as literature, 41–43
ethnohistorical fiction, 43. *See Oficio de tinieblas*
EZLN. *See* Zapatista Army of National Liberation

feminine identity, 94, 103, 104
feminine otherness, 55
femininity, 14; indigenous, 10–11, 82, 85, 86, 101, 103, 104. *See also* Isthmus Zapotec femininity; women
fictional literature. *See* ethnography as literature; narratives
firma, problem of the, 76
First Inter-American Indigenist Conference in Pátzcuaro, Michoacán, 14–16
First Inter-American Indigenous Conference in San Cristóbal de las Casas, 19–20, 73–74
Foundational Fictions (Sommer), 27
foundational indigenista novels, 53–54, 56
foundational myths, 85
Fox, Vicente, 4, 110, 114
Franciscan Monk (Orozco), 98–99
Franco, Jean, 101
Friedlander, Judith, 117n2
functionalist paradigm, 41–42, 44

Gamio, Manuel, 95–96, 102
gay, lesbian, and transgender persons, 82, 84, 89, 90, 100
gender inequality: racial inequality and, 61 (*see also* mestizo nationalism; *Oficio de tinieblas*). *See also* femininity; women
gender roles, 89, 92, 95. *See also* femininity; Juchitán; women
globalization: and challenges of pluriculturalism, 72–74; and rearticulation of indigeneity in Mexico, 5–11
Gosling, Maureen, 87–90. *See also Blossoms of Fire*
Guadalupe, Virgin of, 94, 95

Gutiérrez, Natividad, 92

Hernández, Natalio, 108
Hewitt de Alcántara, Cynthia, 41–42
homosexuality, 82, 84, 89, 90, 100
human rights, 108, 112; human rights abuses by government, 71

incorporation (into "modern civilization"), 16–19, 39. *See also* assimilation
Indian policy, hemisphere-wide, 15
Indian(s), 4, 16; images and stereotypes of, 4, 12–13, 19, 22, 28, 37, 44; as other, 25, 55, 110; self-identification as, 49
indigeneity, 96; defined, 25; emblems of, 113–14; internationalization of the image of, 112; in Mexico, meaning of, 79; between race, class, and culture, 115–16
indigenismo, 110; aim of official, 44; critique of, 18–21, 70–72; definitions and conceptions of, 1–3, 5, 6, 14; ethics of, 19; foundations of official, 14–18; historical perspective on, 14, 24, 80–81; nature of, 12–13, 26; and socialist and capitalist notions of modernity and progress, 62; state-sponsored (from revolution to rehabilitation), 3–4; unraveled, 111–12. *See also specific topics*
indigenista activities, 18; institutions enlisted to serve the aims of, 13
indigenista paradigm, failure of, 107
indigenous cultural identity, new perspectives on, 22
indigenous people's culture, drive to take away, 16
indigenous sovereignty, 6
Institutional Revolutionary Party (PRI), 2, 6, 13, 17, 39, 40, 71, 88; Juchitán and, 88; revolutionary nationalist image, 111–12; state agencies built up around, 110; state-as-benefactor image, 112
Instituto Indigenista Interamericana (III). *See* Inter-American Indigenist Institute
Instituto Nacional de Antropología e Historia (INAH). *See* National Institute of Anthropology and History
Instituto Nacional Indigenista (INI). *See* National Indigenist Institute
intellectuals, 2, 22–24, 62, 68; PRI and, 71
Inter-American Indigenist Conference in Pátzcuaro, Michoacán, 14–16
Inter-American Indigenist Institute (III), 14–16

Inter-American Indigenous Conference of
1974, 19–20, 73–74
International Indigenous Congress, 7
internationalization: of the image of indigeneity, 112. *See also* globalization
Isthmus of Tehuantepec, Oaxaca, 82–86,
90, 100
Isthmus Zapotec artists and writers, 84
Isthmus Zapotec culture and society, 87–90,
96, 97, 102–3; myth of matriarchal
utopia, 86, 100–103; notions of gender
complementarity, 89; social identity in,
89; struggle for self-determination, 90
Isthmus Zapotec exceptionality, myth of,
93, 104
Isthmus Zapotec femininity, 83, 91
Isthmus Zapotec sexuality, 84
Isthmus Zapotec women, 82–85, 87, 88,
100

Jolote, Juan Pérez. *See Juan Pérez Jolote*
journalism, 71
Juan Pérez Jolote (Pozas), 9, 39, 42–49;
compared with *Los hombres verdaderos*, 42,
49–54. *See also* Pozas
Juchitán: engendering, 86–91; struggles for
political autonomy, 88, 89
"Juchitán de las mujeres" (Poniatowska),
87–88
justice, 58

Karttunen, Frances, 100, 122n3

Labyrinth of Solitude, The (Paz), 12, 85, 93
Lacondón Maya, ethnocide and femicide
among, 75–77
Land Distribution for the Indigenous
(resolution), 15–16
land redistribution, 40
land tenure system. *See ejido*
landowners, 17, 58
Lewis, Oscar, 41
liberation movements, 68. *See also* testimonio
Lienhard, Martín, 64
literature, indigenista: conflictive heterogeneity of, 43–54, 63. *See also* ethnography
as literature; narratives; testimonio
Lola Casanova (Rojas González), 35–37
Lomnitz, Claudio, 2, 109
López y Fuentes, Gregorio, 25–26, 28–31;
El indio, 28–31
Los hombres verdaderos (Pozas), 9, 39, 42,
49–54

Los indios en las clases sociales de México (Pozas
and Pozas), 47
love, 26–27

machismo and *machista*, 103
Madrid, Miguel de la, 111
Magdaleno, Mauricio, 31–34
Malinche, 82, 85, 100–103; as conquerable
sign, 91–100; paintings of, 97–98
malinchistas, 100
Marcos, Insurgente, 68, 77–80
marginalization, indigeneity and, 23
Marión, Marie-Odile, 10, 75–77
marketplace of images, indigeneity and the,
113–15
matriarchy, 82, 88
Maya, Lacondón. *See* Lacondón Maya
Mayan language and discourse, 74
media, state control of, 71
Medina, Carlos, 19, 20
mestizaje, 3, 27, 28, 35, 92–94, 99; as antithesis of racist discourses, 92; as cultural
metaphor for citizenship, 96; defined,
13–14; discourse of, 81; gendered, 85;
modernization and, 3, 7, 13–14, 27; as
pharmakos, 100
mestizo culture and society, 9, 10, 13, 17, 41,
44, 46, 84
mestizo (mixed-race), 1, 20, 32, 35–36;
conceptions of, 3, 14, 91, 95; individualistic, 4; as modern citizen, 3; modernity
and, 3, 17
mestizo nationalism, 92, 94–96, 100–103
Mexican Revolution, 14, 40
Mexico City, marketplace of images in,
113–15
migration, internal, 40
Miguel, San, 74
modernization and modernity, 13, 20,
32, 71; mestizaje and, 3, 7, 13–14, 27;
mestizos and, 3, 17
Montemayor, Carlos, 108
Moreiras, Alberto, 62–63
multicultural indigenismo, 115
multiculturalism, 102–3, 112. *See also*
pluriculturalism

narrative transculturation, 50; indigenismo
and, 62–65
narratives, indigenista, 26, 65–66; vicarious
participant observation, 26–38, 41. *See
also* ethnography as literature
National Action Party (PAN), 5, 110

national cohesion, 13
National Council for the Development of
    Indigenous Communities (CONADEPI),
    4–5, 110–11, 116
National Indigenist Institute (INI), 3–5,
    18, 21, 40–41, 72; coordinating centers,
    18, 44; creation of, 16; criticism of, 70;
    inauguration of, 115; and national popular
    state consolidation, 13–14; unraveling and
    cancellation of, 116
National Institute of Anthropology and
    History (INAH), 13
National Museum of Anthropology, 105,
    107, 113
National Peasant Confederation (CNC), 72
National School of Anthropology and
    History (ENAH), 13, 19
national sovereignty, 15
nationalism. *See* mestizo nationalism
neoliberal era, 108; from post-indigenismo
    to pan-indianismo in the, 21–24
North American Free Trade Agreement
    (NAFTA), 5, 6, 22
novels. *See* narratives

Obregón, Álvaro, 17
O'Connell, Joanna, 61–62, 64
Oficio de tinieblas (The True Peoples), 9–10,
    39; as ethnohistorical, 43, 54–62
Orozco, José Clemente, 85, 96–99
otherness, 25, 55, 93

participant observation, 41; vicarious,
    26–38
participatory indigenismo, 108, 115
Partido Acción Nacional (PAN). *See*
    National Action Party
paternalism, 16, 111
patriarchal despotism, 46. *See also Juan Pérez
    Jolote*
patriarchy: caste exploitation and, 55;
    silencing of women in, 59; subjugation of
    women in, 55, 61
Paz, Octavio, 25, 85, 93, 94, 102, 123n5; *The
    Labyrinth of Solitude*, 12
peasant movements, repression of, 20
peasants, 58, 72
Plaza de Tlatelolco, massacre in, 19, 71
pluriculturalism, 81; globalization and chal-
    lenges of, 72–74. *See also* multiculturalism
Polanco, Héctor Díaz, 4
Poniatowska, Elena, 45, 68, 71, 85, 87–88
populism, 17
Portilla, Miguel León, 108

power, language and, 55–56
Pozas, Ricardo, 9, 41, 46, 47; *Juan Pérez Jolote*,
    9, 39, 42–54
PRI. *See* Institutional Revolutionary Party
proto-testimonial narratives, 2. *See also*
    ethnographic coming-of-age stories;
    testimonio; *specific narratives*

¡Que Viva Mexico! (film), 87

racial and gender inequality, 61, 93–94. *See
    also* mestizo nationalism; *Oficio de tinieblas*
Rama, Angel, 63–66
rape: in literature, 28–30, 32, 34, 35, 56, 57;
    of Malinche, 85, 91, 94–95, 101
refuge regions, 18
revolutionary indigenistas, 14
Rivera, Diego, 96, 97, 113
Rojas González, Francisco, 25–26, 34–35;
    Lola Casanova, 35–37
Ros Romero, Consuelo, 19, 20
Rulfo, Juan, 119n11
rural life, 71–72
rural-to-urban migration, 40

Saldaña-Portillo, María Josefina, 95–96,
    102, 103
Salinas de Gortari, Carlos, 5–6, 77
San Andrés Accords, 114
San Juan Chamula. *See Juan Pérez Jolote; Oficio
    de tinieblas*
Sánchez, Consuelo, 17, 108
Seris, 35–37
Serret, Estela, 91
sexuality. *See* eroticism/sexuality
signature, problem of, 76
social inequality, 17–18, 20
Sommer, Doris, 26–27, 34, 66
Spanish language, 74
Spivak, Gayatri Chakravorty, 101
Stavenhagen, Rodolfo, 20
structuralist paradigm, shift from functional
    to, 41–42

testimonio, indigenous, 7, 22–23, 66–70;
    from indigenismo to, 4–5, 7; paradox and
    promise of, 80–81. *See also* indigenismo,
    critique of; proto-testimonial narratives
Tlatelolco, massacre of, 19, 71
transcultural relationships, 55
transculturation, 63; meanings, 62–63. *See
    also* narrative transculturation
transgender persons, 82, 89
Tzeltal culture. *See Los hombres verdaderos*

Tzotzil culture, 61. *See also Juan Pérez Jolote;*
Oficio de tinieblas
Tzotzil-Tzeltal Coordinating Center, 44

urban workers, 40
utopia: erotic, 87. *See also under* Isthmus
Zapotec culture and society

Vasconcelos, José, 93
vela: mayordomos at a, 86; women bearing
gifts at a, 83
Virgin of Guadalupe, 94, 95

wealth, concentration of, 15
welfare state model, dismantling of, 108
Williams, Gareth, 108–9, 112
women (indigenous): bodies, 34; empowerment, 11, 85, 88, 89, 100; good vs. bad,
95; as non-citizens, 103; place in national
society, 1; portrayed in fiction, 34, 61,
62 (*see also Blossoms of Fire*; ethnography as
literature; narratives); representations of,
82; rethinking their agency in postcolonial frame, 100–104; subjugation in
patriarchy, 55, 61 (*see also* patriarchy). *See
also* femininity; *specific topics*
women writers, 62

Zapatismo, 114; and cultural insurgency,
77–80
Zapatista Army of National Liberation
(EZLN), 1, 77–79, 114; demands, 116;
uprising of 1994, 23, 112. *See also* Marcos
Zapatistas, 103
Zapotec women. *See* Isthmus Zapotec
women
Zedillo, Ernesto, 114

About the Author

Analisa Taylor is associate professor of Spanish and Latin American Studies at the University of Oregon. She teaches courses on contemporary Latin America, focusing on Mexican, Central American, and Chicana/o social movements and cultural expression. After studying Spanish and sociology at the University of Oregon and working as a literary translator in Chile, she received her Ph.D. in Spanish and Latin American Studies at Duke University. Her essays have appeared in *Signs: Journal of Women in Culture and Society*, *The Journal of Latin American Cultural Studies*, and *The Latin American Literary Review*.

CPSIA information can be obtained at www.ICGtesting.com
Printed in the USA
LVOW13s1158050813

346297LV00002B/7/P